All's Well That Ends Well by William Shakespeare

The life of William Shakespeare, arguably the most significant figure in the Western literary canon, is relatively unknown.

Shakespeare was born in Stratford-upon-Avon in 1565, possibly on the 23rd April, St. George's Day, and baptised there on 26th April.

Little is known of his education and the first firm facts to his life relate to his marriage, aged 18, to Anne Hathaway, who was 26 and from the nearby village of Shottery. Anne gave birth to their first son six months later.

Shakespeare's first play, The Comedy of Errors began a procession of real heavyweights that were to emanate from his pen in a career of just over twenty years in which 37 plays were written and his reputation forever established.

This early skill was recognised by many and by 1594 the Lord Chamberlain's Men were performing his works. With the advantage of Shakespeare's progressive writing they rapidly became London's leading company of players, affording him more exposure and, following the death of Queen Elizabeth in 1603, a royal patent by the new king, James I, at which point they changed their name to the King's Men.

By 1598, and despite efforts to pirate his work, Shakespeare's name was well known and had become a selling point in its own right on title pages.

No plays are attributed to Shakespeare after 1613, and the last few plays he wrote before this time were in collaboration with other writers, one of whom is likely to be John Fletcher who succeeded him as the house playwright for the King's Men.

William Shakespeare died two months later on April 23rd, 1616, survived by his wife, two daughters and a legacy of writing that none have since yet eclipsed.

Index of Contents
DRAMATIS PERSONAE
ACT I
Scene I - Rousillon. The Count's Palace.
Scene II - Paris. The King's Palace.
Scene III - Rousillon. The Count's Palace.
ACT II
Scene I - Paris. The King's Palace.
Scene II - Rousillon. The Count's Palace.
Scene III - Paris. The King's Palace.
Scene IV - Paris. The King's Palace.
Scene V - Paris. The King's Palace.
ACT III
Scene I - Florence. The Duke's Palace.
Scene II - Rousillon. The Count's Palace.
Scene III - Florence. Before the Duke's Palace.

Scene IV - Rousillon. The Count's Palace.
Scene V - Florence. Without the Walls. A Tucket Afar Off.
Scene VI - Camp Before Florence.
Scene VII - Florence. The Widow's House.
ACT IV
Scene I - Without the Florentine Camp.
Scene II - Florence. The Widow's House.
Scene III - The Florentine Camp.
Scene IV - Florence. The Widow's House.
Scene V - Rousillon. The Count's Palace.
ACT V
Scene I - Marseilles. A Street.
Scene II - Rousillon. Before the Count's Palace.
Scene III - Rousillon. The Count's Palace.
William Shakespeare – A Short Biography
William Shakespeare – A Concise Bibliography
Shakespeare; or, the Poet by Ralph Waldo Emerson
William Shakespeare – A Tribute in Verse

DRAMATIS PERSONAE
KING OF FRANCE
DUKE OF FLORENCE
BERTRAM, Count of Rousillon
COUNTESS OF ROUSILLON, Mother to Bertram
LAVACHE, a Clown in her household
HELENA, a Gentlewoman protected by the Countess
LAFEU, an old Lord
PAROLLES, a follower of Bertram
An Old Widow of Florence
DIANA, Daughter to the Widow
Steward to the Countess of Rousillon
VIOLENTA, MARIANA, Neighbours and Friends to the Widow

SCENE.—Rousillon, Paris, Florence, Marseilles.

ACT I

SCENE I. Rousillon. The Count's Palace.

Enter BERTRAM, the COUNTESS of Rousillon, HELENA, and LAFEU, all in black

COUNTESS
In delivering my son from me, I bury a second husband.

BERTRAM
And I in going, madam, weep o'er my father's death anew: but I must attend his majesty's command, to whom I am now in ward, evermore in subjection.

LAFEU
You shall find of the king a husband, madam; you, sir, a father: he that so generally is at all times good must of necessity hold his virtue to you; whose worthiness would stir it up where it wanted rather than lack it where there is such abundance.

COUNTESS
What hope is there of his majesty's amendment?

LAFEU
He hath abandoned his physicians, madam; under whose practises he hath persecuted time with hope, and finds no other advantage in the process but only the losing of hope by time.

COUNTESS
This young gentlewoman had a father,—O, that 'had'! how sad a passage 'tis!—whose skill was almost as great as his honesty; had it stretched so far, would have made nature immortal, and death should have play for lack of work. Would, for the king's sake, he were living! I think it would be the death of the king's disease.

LAFEU
How called you the man you speak of, madam?

COUNTESS
He was famous, sir, in his profession, and it was his great right to be so: Gerard de Narbon.

LAFEU
He was excellent indeed, madam: the king very lately spoke of him admiringly and mourningly: he was skilful enough to have lived still, if knowledge could be set up against mortality.

BERTRAM
What is it, my good lord, the king languishes of?

LAFEU
A fistula, my lord.

BERTRAM
I heard not of it before.

LAFEU
I would it were not notorious. Was this gentlewoman the daughter of Gerard de Narbon?

COUNTESS
His sole child, my lord, and bequeathed to my overlooking. I have those hopes of her good that her education promises; her dispositions she inherits, which makes fair gifts fairer; for where an unclean mind carries virtuous qualities, there commendations go with pity; they are virtues and traitors too; in her they are the better for their simpleness; she derives her honesty and achieves her goodness.

LAFEU

Your commendations, madam, get from her tears.

COUNTESS
'Tis the best brine a maiden can season her praise in. The remembrance of her father never approaches her heart but the tyranny of her sorrows takes all livelihood from her cheek. No more of this, Helena; go to, no more; lest it be rather thought you affect a sorrow than have it.

HELENA
I do affect a sorrow indeed, but I have it too.

LAFEU
Moderate lamentation is the right of the dead, excessive grief the enemy to the living.

COUNTESS
If the living be enemy to the grief, the excess makes it soon mortal.

BERTRAM
Madam, I desire your holy wishes.

LAFEU
How understand we that?

COUNTESS
Be thou blest, Bertram, and succeed thy father
In manners, as in shape! thy blood and virtue
Contend for empire in thee, and thy goodness
Share with thy birthright! Love all, trust a few,
Do wrong to none: be able for thine enemy
Rather in power than use, and keep thy friend
Under thy own life's key: be cheque'd for silence,
But never tax'd for speech. What heaven more will,
That thee may furnish and my prayers pluck down,
Fall on thy head! Farewell, my lord;
'Tis an unseason'd courtier; good my lord,
Advise him.

LAFEU
He cannot want the best
That shall attend his love.

COUNTESS
Heaven bless him! Farewell, Bertram.

Exit

BERTRAM
[To HELENA] The best wishes that can be forged in your thoughts be servants to you! Be comfortable to my mother, your mistress, and make much of her.

LAFEU
Farewell, pretty lady: you must hold the credit of your father.

Exeunt BERTRAM and LAFEU

HELENA
O, were that all! I think not on my father;
And these great tears grace his remembrance more
Than those I shed for him. What was he like?
I have forgot him: my imagination
Carries no favour in't but Bertram's.
I am undone: there is no living, none,
If Bertram be away. 'Twere all one
That I should love a bright particular star
And think to wed it, he is so above me:
In his bright radiance and collateral light
Must I be comforted, not in his sphere.
The ambition in my love thus plagues itself:
The hind that would be mated by the lion
Must die for love. 'Twas pretty, though plague,
To see him every hour; to sit and draw
His arched brows, his hawking eye, his curls,
In our heart's table; heart too capable
Of every line and trick of his sweet favour:
But now he's gone, and my idolatrous fancy
Must sanctify his reliques. Who comes here?

Enter PAROLLES

Aside

One that goes with him: I love him for his sake;
And yet I know him a notorious liar,
Think him a great way fool, solely a coward;
Yet these fixed evils sit so fit in him,
That they take place, when virtue's steely bones
Look bleak i' the cold wind: withal, full oft we see
Cold wisdom waiting on superfluous folly.

PAROLLES
Save you, fair queen!

HELENA
And you, monarch!

PAROLLES
No.

HELENA
And no.

PAROLLES
Are you meditating on virginity?

HELENA
Ay. You have some stain of soldier in you: let me ask you a question. Man is enemy to virginity; how may we barricado it against him?

PAROLLES
Keep him out.

HELENA
But he assails; and our virginity, though valiant, in the defence yet is weak: unfold to us some warlike resistance.

PAROLLES
There is none: man, sitting down before you, will undermine you and blow you up.

HELENA
Bless our poor virginity from underminers and blowers up! Is there no military policy, how virgins might blow up men?

PAROLLES
Virginity being blown down, man will quicklier be blown up: marry, in blowing him down again, with the breach yourselves made, you lose your city. It is not politic in the commonwealth of nature to preserve virginity. Loss of virginity is rational increase and there was never virgin got till virginity was first lost. That you were made of is metal to make virgins. Virginity by being once lost may be ten times found; by being ever kept, it is ever lost: 'tis too cold a companion; away with 't!

HELENA
I will stand for 't a little, though therefore I die a virgin.

PAROLLES
There's little can be said in 't; 'tis against the rule of nature. To speak on the part of virginity, is to accuse your mothers; which is most infallible disobedience. He that hangs himself is a virgin: virginity murders itself and should be buried in highways out of all sanctified limit, as a desperate offendress against nature. Virginity breeds mites, much like a cheese; consumes itself to the very paring, and so dies with feeding his own stomach. Besides, virginity is peevish, proud, idle, made of self-love, which is the most inhibited sin in the canon. Keep it not; you cannot choose but loose by't: out with 't! within ten year it will make itself ten, which is a goodly increase; and the principal itself not much the worse: away with 't!

HELENA
How might one do, sir, to lose it to her own liking?

PAROLLES
Let me see: marry, ill, to like him that ne'er it likes. 'Tis a commodity will lose the gloss with lying; the longer kept, the less worth: off with ' while 'tis vendible; answer the time of request. Virginity, like an old courtier, wears her cap out of fashion: richly suited, but unsuitable: just like the brooch and the tooth-pick, which wear not now. Your date is better in your pie and your porridge than in your cheek; and your virginity, your old virginity, is like one of our French withered pears, it looks ill, it eats drily; marry, 'tis a withered pear; it was formerly better; marry, yet 'tis a withered pear: will you anything with it?

HELENA
Not my virginity yet
There shall your master have a thousand loves,
A mother and a mistress and a friend,
A phoenix, captain and an enemy,
A guide, a goddess, and a sovereign,
A counsellor, a traitress, and a dear;
His humble ambition, proud humility,
His jarring concord, and his discord dulcet,
His faith, his sweet disaster; with a world
Of pretty, fond, adoptious christendoms,
That blinking Cupid gossips. Now shall he—
I know not what he shall. God send him well!
The court's a learning place, and he is one—

PAROLLES
What one, i' faith?

HELENA
That I wish well. 'Tis pity—

PAROLLES
What's pity?

HELENA
That wishing well had not a body in't,
Which might be felt; that we, the poorer born,
Whose baser stars do shut us up in wishes,
Might with effects of them follow our friends,
And show what we alone must think, which never
Return us thanks.

Enter PAGE

PAGE
Monsieur Parolles, my lord calls for you.

Exit

PAROLLES
Little Helen, farewell; if I can remember thee, I will think of thee at court.

HELENA
Monsieur Parolles, you were born under a charitable star.

PAROLLES
Under Mars, I.

HELENA
I especially think, under Mars.

PAROLLES
Why under Mars?

HELENA
The wars have so kept you under that you must needs be born under Mars.

PAROLLES
When he was predominant.

HELENA
When he was retrograde, I think, rather.

PAROLLES
Why think you so?

HELENA
You go so much backward when you fight.

PAROLLES
That's for advantage.

HELENA
So is running away, when fear proposes the safety; but the composition that your valour and fear makes in you is a virtue of a good wing, and I like the wear well.

PAROLLES
I am so full of businesses, I cannot answer thee acutely. I will return perfect courtier; in the which, my instruction shall serve to naturalize thee, so thou wilt be capable of a courtier's counsel and understand what advice shall thrust upon thee; else thou diest in thine unthankfulness, and thine ignorance makes thee away: farewell. When thou hast leisure, say thy prayers; when thou hast none, remember thy friends; get thee a good husband, and use him as he uses thee; so, farewell.

Exit

HELENA
Our remedies oft in ourselves do lie,
Which we ascribe to heaven: the fated sky
Gives us free scope, only doth backward pull
Our slow designs when we ourselves are dull.
What power is it which mounts my love so high,
That makes me see, and cannot feed mine eye?
The mightiest space in fortune nature brings
To join like likes and kiss like native things.
Impossible be strange attempts to those
That weigh their pains in sense and do suppose
What hath been cannot be: who ever strove
So show her merit, that did miss her love?
The king's disease—my project may deceive me,
But my intents are fix'd and will not leave me.

Exit

SCENE II. Paris. The KING's palace.
Flourish of cornets. Enter the KING of France, with letters, and divers Attendants

KING
The Florentines and Senoys are by the ears;
Have fought with equal fortune and continue
A braving war.

First Lord
So 'tis reported, sir.

KING
Nay, 'tis most credible; we here received it
A certainty, vouch'd from our cousin Austria,
With caution that the Florentine will move us
For speedy aid; wherein our dearest friend
Prejudicates the business and would seem
To have us make denial.

First Lord
His love and wisdom,
Approved so to your majesty, may plead
For amplest credence.

KING
He hath arm'd our answer,
And Florence is denied before he comes:
Yet, for our gentlemen that mean to see
The Tuscan service, freely have they leave
To stand on either part.

Second Lord
It well may serve
A nursery to our gentry, who are sick
For breathing and exploit.

KING
What's he comes here?

Enter BERTRAM, LAFEU, and PAROLLES

First Lord
It is the Count Rousillon, my good lord,
Young Bertram.

KING
Youth, thou bear'st thy father's face;
Frank nature, rather curious than in haste,

Hath well composed thee. Thy father's moral parts
Mayst thou inherit too! Welcome to Paris.

BERTRAM
My thanks and duty are your majesty's.

KING
I would I had that corporal soundness now,
As when thy father and myself in friendship
First tried our soldiership! He did look far
Into the service of the time and was
Discipled of the bravest: he lasted long;
But on us both did haggish age steal on
And wore us out of act. It much repairs me
To talk of your good father. In his youth
He had the wit which I can well observe
To-day in our young lords; but they may jest
Till their own scorn return to them unnoted
Ere they can hide their levity in honour;
So like a courtier, contempt nor bitterness
Were in his pride or sharpness; if they were,
His equal had awaked them, and his honour,
Clock to itself, knew the true minute when
Exception bid him speak, and at this time
His tongue obey'd his hand: who were below him
He used as creatures of another place
And bow'd his eminent top to their low ranks,
Making them proud of his humility,
In their poor praise he humbled. Such a man
Might be a copy to these younger times;
Which, follow'd well, would demonstrate them now
But goers backward.

BERTRAM
His good remembrance, sir,
Lies richer in your thoughts than on his tomb;
So in approof lives not his epitaph
As in your royal speech.

KING
Would I were with him! He would always say—
Methinks I hear him now; his plausive words
He scatter'd not in ears, but grafted them,
To grow there and to bear,—'Let me not live,'—
This his good melancholy oft began,
On the catastrophe and heel of pastime,
When it was out,—'Let me not live,' quoth he,
'After my flame lacks oil, to be the snuff
Of younger spirits, whose apprehensive senses
All but new things disdain; whose judgments are
Mere fathers of their garments; whose constancies

Expire before their fashions.' This he wish'd;
I after him do after him wish too,
Since I nor wax nor honey can bring home,
I quickly were dissolved from my hive,
To give some labourers room.

SECOND LORD
You are loved, sir:
They that least lend it you shall lack you first.

KING
I fill a place, I know't. How long is't, count,
Since the physician at your father's died?
He was much famed.

BERTRAM
Some six months since, my lord.

KING
If he were living, I would try him yet.
Lend me an arm; the rest have worn me out
With several applications; nature and sickness
Debate it at their leisure. Welcome, count;
My son's no dearer.

BERTRAM
Thank your majesty.

Exeunt. Flourish

SCENE III. Rousillon. The Count's Palace.

Enter COUNTESS, STEWARD, and CLOWN

COUNTESS
I will now hear; what say you of this gentlewoman?

STEWARD
Madam, the care I have had to even your content, I wish might be found in the calendar of my past endeavours; for then we wound our modesty and make foul the clearness of our deservings, when of ourselves we publish them.

COUNTESS
What does this knave here? Get you gone, sirrah: the complaints I have heard of you I do not all believe: 'tis my slowness that I do not; for I know you lack not folly to commit them, and have ability enough to make such knaveries yours.

CLOWN
'Tis not unknown to you, madam, I am a poor fellow.

COUNTESS
Well, sir.

CLOWN
No, madam, 'tis not so well that I am poor, though many of the rich are damned: but, if I may have your ladyship's good will to go to the world, Isbel the woman and I will do as we may.

COUNTESS
Wilt thou needs be a beggar?

CLOWN
I do beg your good will in this case.

COUNTESS
In what case?

CLOWN
In Isbel's case and mine own. Service is no heritage: and I think I shall never have the blessing of God till I have issue o' my body; for they say barnes are blessings.

COUNTESS
Tell me thy reason why thou wilt marry.

CLOWN
My poor body, madam, requires it: I am driven on by the flesh; and he must needs go that the devil drives.

COUNTESS
Is this all your worship's reason?

CLOWN
Faith, madam, I have other holy reasons such as they are.

COUNTESS
May the world know them?

CLOWN
I have been, madam, a wicked creature, as you and all flesh and blood are; and, indeed, I do marry that I may repent.

COUNTESS
Thy marriage, sooner than thy wickedness.

CLOWN
I am out o' friends, madam; and I hope to have friends for my wife's sake.

COUNTESS
Such friends are thine enemies, knave.

CLOWN

You're shallow, madam, in great friends; for the knaves come to do that for me which I am aweary of. He that ears my land spares my team and gives me leave to in the crop; if I be his cuckold, he's my drudge: he that comforts my wife is the cherisher of my flesh and blood; he that cherishes my flesh and blood loves my flesh and blood; he that loves my flesh and blood is my friend: ergo, he that kisses my wife is my friend. If men could be contented to be what they are, there were no fear in marriage; for young Charbon the Puritan and old Poysam the Papist, howsome'er their hearts are severed in religion, their heads are both one; they may jowl horns together, like any deer i' the herd.

COUNTESS
Wilt thou ever be a foul-mouthed and calumnious knave?

CLOWN
A prophet I, madam; and I speak the truth the next way:
For I the ballad will repeat,
Which men full true shall find;
Your marriage comes by destiny,
Your cuckoo sings by kind.

COUNTESS
Get you gone, sir; I'll talk with you more anon.

STEWARD
May it please you, madam, that he bid Helen come to you: of her I am to speak.

COUNTESS
Sirrah, tell my gentlewoman I would speak with her; Helen, I mean.

CLOWN
Was this fair face the cause, quoth she,
Why the Grecians sacked Troy?
Fond done, done fond,
Was this King Priam's joy?
With that she sighed as she stood,
With that she sighed as she stood,
And gave this sentence then;
Among nine bad if one be good,
Among nine bad if one be good,
There's yet one good in ten.

COUNTESS
What, one good in ten? you corrupt the song, sirrah.

CLOWN
One good woman in ten, madam; which is a purifying o' the song: would God would serve the world so all the year! we'ld find no fault with the tithe-woman, if I were the parson. One in ten, quoth a'! An we might have a good woman born but one every blazing star, or at an earthquake, 'twould Mend the lottery well: a man may draw his heart out, ere a' pluck one.

COUNTESS
You'll be gone, sir knave, and do as I command you.

Clown
That man should be at woman's command, and yet no hurt done! Though honesty be no puritan, yet it will do no hurt; it will wear the surplice of humility over the black gown of a big heart. I am going, forsooth: the business is for Helen to come hither.

Exit

COUNTESS
Well, now.

STEWARD
I know, madam, you love your gentlewoman entirely.

COUNTESS
Faith, I do: her father bequeathed her to me; and she herself, without other advantage, may lawfully make title to as much love as she finds: there is more owing her than is paid; and more shall be paid her than she'll demand.

STEWARD
Madam, I was very late more near her than I think she wished me: alone she was, and did communicate to herself her own words to her own ears; she thought, I dare vow for her, they touched not any stranger sense. Her matter was, she loved your son: Fortune, she said, was no goddess, that had put such difference betwixt their two estates; Love no god, that would not extend his might, only where qualities were level; Dian no queen of virgins, that would suffer her poor knight surprised, without rescue in the first assault or ransom afterward. This she delivered in the most bitter touch of sorrow that e'er I heard virgin exclaim in: which I held my duty speedily to acquaint you withal; sithence, in the loss that may happen, it concerns you something to know it.

COUNTESS
You have discharged this honestly; keep it to yourself: many likelihoods informed me of this before, which hung so tottering in the balance that I could neither believe nor misdoubt. Pray you, leave me: stall this in your bosom; and I thank you for your honest care: I will speak with you further anon.

Exit STEWARD

Enter HELENA

Even so it was with me when I was young:
If ever we are nature's, these are ours; this thorn
Doth to our rose of youth rightly belong;
Our blood to us, this to our blood is born;
It is the show and seal of nature's truth,
Where love's strong passion is impress'd in youth:
By our remembrances of days foregone,
Such were our faults, or then we thought them none.
Her eye is sick on't: I observe her now.

HELENA
What is your pleasure, madam?

COUNTESS
You know, Helen,
I am a mother to you.

HELENA
Mine honourable mistress.

COUNTESS
Nay, a mother:
Why not a mother? When I said 'a mother,'
Methought you saw a serpent: what's in 'mother,'
That you start at it? I say, I am your mother;
And put you in the catalogue of those
That were enwombed mine: 'tis often seen
Adoption strives with nature and choice breeds
A native slip to us from foreign seeds:
You ne'er oppress'd me with a mother's groan,
Yet I express to you a mother's care:
God's mercy, maiden! does it curd thy blood
To say I am thy mother? What's the matter,
That this distemper'd messenger of wet,
The many-colour'd Iris, rounds thine eye?
Why? that you are my daughter?

HELENA
That I am not.

COUNTESS
I say, I am your mother.

HELENA
Pardon, madam;
The Count Rousillon cannot be my brother:
I am from humble, he from honour'd name;
No note upon my parents, his all noble:
My master, my dear lord he is; and I
His servant live, and will his vassal die:
He must not be my brother.

COUNTESS
Nor I your mother?

HELENA
You are my mother, madam; would you were,—
So that my lord your son were not my brother,—
Indeed my mother! or were you both our mothers,
I care no more for than I do for heaven,
So I were not his sister. Can't no other,
But, I your daughter, he must be my brother?

COUNTESS

Yes, Helen, you might be my daughter-in-law:
God shield you mean it not! daughter and mother
So strive upon your pulse. What, pale again?
My fear hath catch'd your fondness: now I see
The mystery of your loneliness, and find
Your salt tears' head: now to all sense 'tis gross
You love my son; invention is ashamed,
Against the proclamation of thy passion,
To say thou dost not: therefore tell me true;
But tell me then, 'tis so; for, look thy cheeks
Confess it, th' one to th' other; and thine eyes
See it so grossly shown in thy behaviors
That in their kind they speak it: only sin
And hellish obstinacy tie thy tongue,
That truth should be suspected. Speak, is't so?
If it be so, you have wound a goodly clew;
If it be not, forswear't: howe'er, I charge thee,
As heaven shall work in me for thine avail,
Tell me truly.

HELENA
Good madam, pardon me!

COUNTESS
Do you love my son?

HELENA
Your pardon, noble mistress!

COUNTESS
Love you my son?

HELENA
Do not you love him, madam?

COUNTESS
Go not about; my love hath in't a bond,
Whereof the world takes note: come, come, disclose
The state of your affection; for your passions
Have to the full appeach'd.

HELENA
Then, I confess,
Here on my knee, before high heaven and you,
That before you, and next unto high heaven,
I love your son.
My friends were poor, but honest; so's my love:
Be not offended; for it hurts not him
That he is loved of me: I follow him not
By any token of presumptuous suit;
Nor would I have him till I do deserve him;

Yet never know how that desert should be.
I know I love in vain, strive against hope;
Yet in this captious and intenible sieve
I still pour in the waters of my love
And lack not to lose still: thus, Indian-like,
Religious in mine error, I adore
The sun, that looks upon his worshipper,
But knows of him no more. My dearest madam,
Let not your hate encounter with my love
For loving where you do: but if yourself,
Whose aged honour cites a virtuous youth,
Did ever in so true a flame of liking
Wish chastely and love dearly, that your Dian
Was both herself and love: O, then, give pity
To her, whose state is such that cannot choose
But lend and give where she is sure to lose;
That seeks not to find that her search implies,
But riddle-like lives sweetly where she dies!

COUNTESS
Had you not lately an intent,—speak truly,—
To go to Paris?

HELENA
Madam, I had.

COUNTESS
Wherefore? tell true.

HELENA
I will tell truth; by grace itself I swear.
You know my father left me some prescriptions
Of rare and proved effects, such as his reading
And manifest experience had collected
For general sovereignty; and that he will'd me
In heedfull'st reservation to bestow them,
As notes whose faculties inclusive were
More than they were in note: amongst the rest,
There is a remedy, approved, set down,
To cure the desperate languishings whereof
The king is render'd lost.

COUNTESS
This was your motive
For Paris, was it? speak.

HELENA
My lord your son made me to think of this;
Else Paris and the medicine and the king
Had from the conversation of my thoughts
Haply been absent then.

COUNTESS
But think you, Helen,
If you should tender your supposed aid,
He would receive it? he and his physicians
Are of a mind; he, that they cannot help him,
They, that they cannot help: how shall they credit
A poor unlearned virgin, when the schools,
Embowell'd of their doctrine, have left off
The danger to itself?

HELENA
There's something in't,
More than my father's skill, which was the greatest
Of his profession, that his good receipt
Shall for my legacy be sanctified

By the luckiest stars in heaven: and, would your honour
But give me leave to try success, I'ld venture
The well-lost life of mine on his grace's cure
By such a day and hour.

COUNTESS
Dost thou believe't?

HELENA
Ay, madam, knowingly.

COUNTESS
Why, Helen, thou shalt have my leave and love,
Means and attendants and my loving greetings
To those of mine in court: I'll stay at home
And pray God's blessing into thy attempt:
Be gone to-morrow; and be sure of this,
What I can help thee to thou shalt not miss.

Exeunt

ACT II

SCENE I. Paris. The King's Palace.

Flourish of cornets. Enter the KING, attended with diverse young LORDS taking leave for the Florentine war; BERTRAM, and PAROLLES

KING
Farewell, young lords; these warlike principles
Do not throw from you: and you, my lords, farewell:
Share the advice betwixt you; if both gain, all

The gift doth stretch itself as 'tis received,
And is enough for both.

FIRST LORD
'Tis our hope, sir,
After well enter'd soldiers, to return
And find your grace in health.

KING
No, no, it cannot be; and yet my heart
Will not confess he owes the malady
That doth my life besiege. Farewell, young lords;
Whether I live or die, be you the sons
Of worthy Frenchmen: let higher Italy,—
Those bated that inherit but the fall
Of the last monarchy,—see that you come
Not to woo honour, but to wed it; when
The bravest questant shrinks, find what you seek,
That fame may cry you loud: I say, farewell.

SECOND LORD
Health, at your bidding, serve your majesty!

KING
Those girls of Italy, take heed of them:
They say, our French lack language to deny,
If they demand: beware of being captives,
Before you serve.

BOTH
Our hearts receive your warnings.

KING
Farewell. Come hither to me.

Exit, attended

FIRST LORD
O, my sweet lord, that you will stay behind us!

PAROLLES
'Tis not his fault, the spark.

SECOND LORD
O, 'tis brave wars!

PAROLLES
Most admirable: I have seen those wars.

BERTRAM

I am commanded here, and kept a coil with
'Too young' and 'the next year' and ''tis too early.'

PAROLLES
An thy mind stand to't, boy, steal away bravely.

BERTRAM
I shall stay here the forehorse to a smock,
Creaking my shoes on the plain masonry,
Till honour be bought up and no sword worn
But one to dance with! By heaven, I'll steal away.

FIRST LORD
There's honour in the theft.

PAROLLES
Commit it, count.

SECOND LORD
I am your accessary; and so, farewell.

BERTRAM
I grow to you, and our parting is a tortured body.

FIRST LORD
Farewell, captain.

SECOND LORD
Sweet Monsieur Parolles!

PAROLLES
Noble heroes, my sword and yours are kin. Good sparks and lustrous, a word, good metals: you shall find in the regiment of the Spinii one Captain Spurio, with his cicatrice, an emblem of war, here on his sinister cheek; it was this very sword entrenched it: say to him, I live; and observe his reports for me.

FIRST LORD
We shall, noble captain.

Exeunt LORDS

PAROLLES
Mars dote on you for his novices! what will ye do?

BERTRAM
Stay: the king.

Re-enter KING. BERTRAM and PAROLLES retire

PAROLLES

[To BERTRAM] Use a more spacious ceremony to the noble lords; you have restrained yourself within the list of too cold an adieu: be more expressive to them: for they wear themselves in the cap of the time, there do muster true gait, eat, speak, and move under the influence of the most received star; and though the devil lead the measure, such are to be followed: after them, and take a more dilated farewell.

BERTRAM
And I will do so.

PAROLLES
Worthy fellows; and like to prove most sinewy sword-men.

Exeunt BERTRAM and PAROLLES

Enter LAFEU

LAFEU
[Kneeling] Pardon, my lord, for me and for my tidings.

KING
I'll fee thee to stand up.

LAFEU
Then here's a man stands, that has brought his pardon.
I would you had kneel'd, my lord, to ask me mercy,
And that at my bidding you could so stand up.

KING
I would I had; so I had broke thy pate,
And ask'd thee mercy for't.

LAFEU
Good faith, across: but, my good lord 'tis thus;
Will you be cured of your infirmity?

KING
No.

LAFEU
O, will you eat no grapes, my royal fox?
Yes, but you will my noble grapes, an if
My royal fox could reach them: I have seen a medicine
That's able to breathe life into a stone,
Quicken a rock, and make you dance canary
With spritely fire and motion; whose simple touch,
Is powerful to araise King Pepin, nay,
To give great Charlemain a pen in's hand,
And write to her a love-line.

KING
What 'her' is this?

LAFEU
Why, Doctor She: my lord, there's one arrived,
If you will see her: now, by my faith and honour,
If seriously I may convey my thoughts
In this my light deliverance, I have spoke
With one that, in her sex, her years, profession,
Wisdom and constancy, hath amazed me more
Than I dare blame my weakness: will you see her
For that is her demand, and know her business?
That done, laugh well at me.

KING
Now, good Lafeu,
Bring in the admiration; that we with thee
May spend our wonder too, or take off thine
By wondering how thou took'st it.

LAFEU
Nay, I'll fit you,
And not be all day neither.

Exit

KING
Thus he his special nothing ever prologues.

Re-enter LAFEU, with HELENA

LAFEU
Nay, come your ways.

KING
This haste hath wings indeed.

LAFEU
Nay, come your ways:
This is his majesty; say your mind to him:
A traitor you do look like; but such traitors
His majesty seldom fears: I am Cressid's uncle,
That dare leave two together; fare you well.

Exit

KING
Now, fair one, does your business follow us?

HELENA
Ay, my good lord.
Gerard de Narbon was my father;
In what he did profess, well found.

KING
I knew him.

HELENA
The rather will I spare my praises towards him:
Knowing him is enough. On's bed of death
Many receipts he gave me: chiefly one.
Which, as the dearest issue of his practise,
And of his old experience the oily darling,
He bade me store up, as a triple eye,
Safer than mine own two, more dear; I have so;
And hearing your high majesty is touch'd
With that malignant cause wherein the honour
Of my dear father's gift stands chief in power,
I come to tender it and my appliance
With all bound humbleness.

KING
We thank you, maiden;
But may not be so credulous of cure,
When our most learned doctors leave us and
The congregated college have concluded
That labouring art can never ransom nature
From her inaidible estate; I say we must not
So stain our judgment, or corrupt our hope,
To prostitute our past-cure malady
To empirics, or to dissever so
Our great self and our credit, to esteem
A senseless help when help past sense we deem.

HELENA
My duty then shall pay me for my pains:
I will no more enforce mine office on you.
Humbly entreating from your royal thoughts
A modest one, to bear me back again.

KING
I cannot give thee less, to be call'd grateful:
Thou thought'st to help me; and such thanks I give
As one near death to those that wish him live:
But what at full I know, thou know'st no part,
I knowing all my peril, thou no art.

HELENA
What I can do can do no hurt to try,
Since you set up your rest 'gainst remedy.
He that of greatest works is finisher
Oft does them by the weakest minister:
So holy writ in babes hath judgment shown,
When judges have been babes; great floods have flown

From simple sources, and great seas have dried
When miracles have by the greatest been denied.
Oft expectation fails and most oft there
Where most it promises, and oft it hits
Where hope is coldest and despair most fits.

KING
I must not hear thee; fare thee well, kind maid;
Thy pains not used must by thyself be paid:
Proffers not took reap thanks for their reward.

HELENA
Inspired merit so by breath is barr'd:
It is not so with Him that all things knows
As 'tis with us that square our guess by shows;
But most it is presumption in us when
The help of heaven we count the act of men.
Dear sir, to my endeavours give consent;
Of heaven, not me, make an experiment.
I am not an impostor that proclaim
Myself against the level of mine aim;
But know I think and think I know most sure
My art is not past power nor you past cure.

KING
Are thou so confident? within what space
Hopest thou my cure?

HELENA
The great'st grace lending grace
Ere twice the horses of the sun shall bring
Their fiery torcher his diurnal ring,
Ere twice in murk and occidental damp
Moist Hesperus hath quench'd his sleepy lamp,
Or four and twenty times the pilot's glass
Hath told the thievish minutes how they pass,
What is infirm from your sound parts shall fly,
Health shall live free and sickness freely die.

KING
Upon thy certainty and confidence
What darest thou venture?

HELENA
Tax of impudence,
A strumpet's boldness, a divulged shame
Traduced by odious ballads: my maiden's name
Sear'd otherwise; nay, worse—if worse—extended
With vilest torture let my life be ended.

KING

Methinks in thee some blessed spirit doth speak
His powerful sound within an organ weak:
And what impossibility would slay
In common sense, sense saves another way.
Thy life is dear; for all that life can rate
Worth name of life in thee hath estimate,
Youth, beauty, wisdom, courage, all
That happiness and prime can happy call:
Thou this to hazard needs must intimate
Skill infinite or monstrous desperate.
Sweet practiser, thy physic I will try,
That ministers thine own death if I die.

HELENA
If I break time, or flinch in property
Of what I spoke, unpitied let me die,
And well deserved: not helping, death's my fee;
But, if I help, what do you promise me?

KING
Make thy demand.

HELENA
But will you make it even?

KING
Ay, by my sceptre and my hopes of heaven.

HELENA
Then shalt thou give me with thy kingly hand
What husband in thy power I will command:
Exempted be from me the arrogance
To choose from forth the royal blood of France,
My low and humble name to propagate
With any branch or image of thy state;
But such a one, thy vassal, whom I know
Is free for me to ask, thee to bestow.

KING
Here is my hand; the premises observed,
Thy will by my performance shall be served:
So make the choice of thy own time, for I,
Thy resolved patient, on thee still rely.
More should I question thee, and more I must,
Though more to know could not be more to trust,
From whence thou camest, how tended on: but rest
Unquestion'd welcome and undoubted blest.
Give me some help here, ho! If thou proceed
As high as word, my deed shall match thy meed.

Flourish. Exeunt

SCENE II. Rousillon. The Count's Palace.

Enter COUNTESS and CLOWN

COUNTESS
Come on, sir; I shall now put you to the height of your breeding.

CLOWN
I will show myself highly fed and lowly taught: I know my business is but to the court.

COUNTESS
To the court! why, what place make you special, when you put off that with such contempt? But to the court!

CLOWN
Truly, madam, if God have lent a man any manners, he may easily put it off at court: he that cannot make a leg, put off's cap, kiss his hand and say nothing, has neither leg, hands, lip, nor cap; and indeed such a fellow, to say precisely, were not for the court; but for me, I have an answer will serve all men.

COUNTESS
Marry, that's a bountiful answer that fits all questions.

CLOWN
It is like a barber's chair that fits all buttocks, the pin-buttock, the quatch-buttock, the brawn buttock, or any buttock.

COUNTESS
Will your answer serve fit to all questions?

CLOWN
As fit as ten groats is for the hand of an attorney, as your French crown for your taffeta punk, as Tib's rush for Tom's forefinger, as a pancake for Shrove Tuesday, a morris for May-day, as the nail to his hole, the cuckold to his horn, as a scolding queen to a wrangling knave, as the nun's lip to the friar's mouth, nay, as the pudding to his skin.

COUNTESS
Have you, I say, an answer of such fitness for all questions?

CLOWN
From below your duke to beneath your constable, it will fit any question.

COUNTESS
It must be an answer of most monstrous size that must fit all demands.

CLOWN
But a trifle neither, in good faith, if the learned should speak truth of it: here it is, and all that belongs to't. Ask me if I am a courtier: it shall do you no harm to learn.

COUNTESS
To be young again, if we could: I will be a fool in question, hoping to be the wiser by your answer. I pray you, sir, are you a courtier?

CLOWN
O Lord, sir! There's a simple putting off. More, more, a hundred of them.

COUNTESS
Sir, I am a poor friend of yours, that loves you.

CLOWN
O Lord, sir! Thick, thick, spare not me.

COUNTESS
I think, sir, you can eat none of this homely meat.

CLOWN
O Lord, sir! Nay, put me to't, I warrant you.

COUNTESS
You were lately whipped, sir, as I think.

CLOWN
O Lord, sir! spare not me.

COUNTESS
Do you cry, 'O Lord, sir!' at your whipping, and 'spare not me?' Indeed your 'O Lord, sir!' is very sequent to your whipping: you would answer very well to a whipping, if you were but bound to't.

CLOWN
I ne'er had worse luck in my life in my 'O Lord, sir!' I see things may serve long, but not serve ever.

COUNTESS
I play the noble housewife with the time
To entertain't so merrily with a fool.

Clown
O Lord, sir! why, there't serves well again.

COUNTESS
An end, sir; to your business. Give Helen this,
And urge her to a present answer back:
Commend me to my kinsmen and my son:
This is not much.

CLOWN
Not much commendation to them.

COUNTESS
Not much employment for you: you understand me?

Clown
Most fruitfully: I am there before my legs.

COUNTESS
Haste you again.

Exeunt severally

SCENE III. Paris. The King's Palace.

Enter BERTRAM, LAFEU, and PAROLLES

LAFEU
They say miracles are past; and we have our philosophical persons, to make modern and familiar, things supernatural and causeless. Hence is it that we make trifles of terrors, ensconcing ourselves into seeming knowledge, when we should submit ourselves to an unknown fear.

PAROLLES
Why, 'tis the rarest argument of wonder that hath shot out in our latter times.

BERTRAM
And so 'tis.

LAFEU
To be relinquish'd of the artists,—

PAROLLES
So I say.

LAFEU
Both of Galen and Paracelsus.

PAROLLES
So I say.

LAFEU
Of all the learned and authentic fellows,—

PAROLLES
Right; so I say.

LAFEU
That gave him out incurable,—

PAROLLES
Why, there 'tis; so say I too.

LAFEU

Not to be helped,—

PAROLLES
Right; as 'twere, a man assured of a—

LAFEU
Uncertain life, and sure death.

PAROLLES
Just, you say well; so would I have said.

LAFEU
I may truly say, it is a novelty to the world.

PAROLLES
It is, indeed: if you will have it in showing, you shall read it in—what do you call there?

LAFEU
A showing of a heavenly effect in an earthly actor.

PAROLLES
That's it; I would have said the very same.

LAFEU
Why, your dolphin is not lustier: 'fore me,
I speak in respect—

PAROLLES
Nay, 'tis strange, 'tis very strange, that is the brief and the tedious of it; and he's of a most facinerious spirit that will not acknowledge it to be the—

LAFEU
Very hand of heaven.

PAROLLES
Ay, so I say.

LAFEU
In a most weak—

Pausing

and debile minister, great power, great transcendence: which should, indeed, give us a further use to be made than alone the recovery of the king, as to be—

pausing

generally thankful.

PAROLLES
I would have said it; you say well. Here comes the king.

Enter KING, HELENA, and Attendants. LAFEU and PAROLLES retire

LAFEU
Lustig, as the Dutchman says: I'll like a maid the better, whilst I have a tooth in my head: why, he's able to lead her a coranto.

PAROLLES
Mort du vinaigre! is not this Helen?

LAFEU
'Fore God, I think so.

KING
Go, call before me all the lords in court.
Sit, my preserver, by thy patient's side;
And with this healthful hand, whose banish'd sense
Thou hast repeal'd, a second time receive
The confirmation of my promised gift,
Which but attends thy naming.

Enter three or four LORDS

Fair maid, send forth thine eye: this youthful parcel
Of noble bachelors stand at my bestowing,
O'er whom both sovereign power and father's voice
I have to use: thy frank election make;
Thou hast power to choose, and they none to forsake.

HELENA
To each of you one fair and virtuous mistress
Fall, when Love please! marry, to each, but one!

LAFEU
I'ld give bay Curtal and his furniture,
My mouth no more were broken than these boys',
And writ as little beard.

KING
Peruse them well:
Not one of those but had a noble father.

HELENA
Gentlemen,
Heaven hath through me restored the king to health.

ALL
We understand it, and thank heaven for you.

HELENA

I am a simple maid, and therein wealthiest,
That I protest I simply am a maid.
Please it your majesty, I have done already:
The blushes in my cheeks thus whisper me,
'We blush that thou shouldst choose; but, be refused,
Let the white death sit on thy cheek for ever;
We'll ne'er come there again.'

KING
Make choice; and, see,
Who shuns thy love shuns all his love in me.

HELENA
Now, Dian, from thy altar do I fly,
And to imperial Love, that god most high,
Do my sighs stream. Sir, will you hear my suit?

FIRST LORD
And grant it.

HELENA
Thanks, sir; all the rest is mute.

LAFEU
I had rather be in this choice than throw ames-ace for my life.

HELENA
The honour, sir, that flames in your fair eyes,
Before I speak, too threateningly replies:
Love make your fortunes twenty times above
Her that so wishes and her humble love!

SECOND LORD
No better, if you please.

HELENA
My wish receive,
Which great Love grant! and so, I take my leave.

LAFEU
Do all they deny her? An they were sons of mine,
I'd have them whipped; or I would send them to the
Turk, to make eunuchs of.

HELENA
Be not afraid that I your hand should take;
I'll never do you wrong for your own sake:
Blessing upon your vows! and in your bed
Find fairer fortune, if you ever wed!

LAFEU
These boys are boys of ice, they'll none have her: sure, they are bastards to the English; the French ne'er got 'em.

HELENA
You are too young, too happy, and too good,
To make yourself a son out of my blood.

FOURTH LORD
Fair one, I think not so.

LAFEU
There's one grape yet; I am sure thy father drunk wine: but if thou be'st not an ass, I am a youth of fourteen; I have known thee already.

HELENA
[To BERTRAM] I dare not say I take you; but I give
Me and my service, ever whilst I live,
Into your guiding power. This is the man.

KING
Why, then, young Bertram, take her; she's thy wife.

BERTRAM
My wife, my liege! I shall beseech your highness,
In such a business give me leave to use
The help of mine own eyes.

KING
Know'st thou not, Bertram,
What she has done for me?

BERTRAM
Yes, my good lord;
But never hope to know why I should marry her.

KING
Thou know'st she has raised me from my sickly bed.

BERTRAM
But follows it, my lord, to bring me down
Must answer for your raising? I know her well:
She had her breeding at my father's charge.
A poor physician's daughter my wife! Disdain
Rather corrupt me ever!

KING
'Tis only title thou disdain'st in her, the which
I can build up. Strange is it that our bloods,
Of colour, weight, and heat, pour'd all together,
Would quite confound distinction, yet stand off

In differences so mighty. If she be
All that is virtuous, save what thou dislikest,
A poor physician's daughter, thou dislikest
Of virtue for the name: but do not so:
From lowest place when virtuous things proceed,
The place is dignified by the doer's deed:
Where great additions swell's, and virtue none,
It is a dropsied honour. Good alone
Is good without a name. Vileness is so:
The property by what it is should go,
Not by the title. She is young, wise, fair;
In these to nature she's immediate heir,
And these breed honour: that is honour's scorn,
Which challenges itself as honour's born
And is not like the sire: honours thrive,
When rather from our acts we them derive
Than our foregoers: the mere word's a slave
Debosh'd on every tomb, on every grave
A lying trophy, and as oft is dumb
Where dust and damn'd oblivion is the tomb
Of honour'd bones indeed. What should be said?
If thou canst like this creature as a maid,
I can create the rest: virtue and she
Is her own dower; honour and wealth from me.

BERTRAM
I cannot love her, nor will strive to do't.

KING
Thou wrong'st thyself, if thou shouldst strive to choose.

HELENA
That you are well restored, my lord, I'm glad:
Let the rest go.

KING
My honour's at the stake; which to defeat,
I must produce my power. Here, take her hand,
Proud scornful boy, unworthy this good gift;
That dost in vile misprision shackle up
My love and her desert; that canst not dream,
We, poising us in her defective scale,
Shall weigh thee to the beam; that wilt not know,
It is in us to plant thine honour where
We please to have it grow. Cheque thy contempt:
Obey our will, which travails in thy good:
Believe not thy disdain, but presently
Do thine own fortunes that obedient right
Which both thy duty owes and our power claims;
Or I will throw thee from my care for ever
Into the staggers and the careless lapse

Of youth and ignorance; both my revenge and hate
Loosing upon thee, in the name of justice,
Without all terms of pity. Speak; thine answer.

BERTRAM
Pardon, my gracious lord; for I submit
My fancy to your eyes: when I consider
What great creation and what dole of honour
Flies where you bid it, I find that she, which late
Was in my nobler thoughts most base, is now
The praised of the king; who, so ennobled,
Is as 'twere born so.

KING
Take her by the hand,
And tell her she is thine: to whom I promise
A counterpoise, if not to thy estate
A balance more replete.

BERTRAM
I take her hand.

KING
Good fortune and the favour of the king
Smile upon this contract; whose ceremony
Shall seem expedient on the now-born brief,
And be perform'd to-night: the solemn feast
Shall more attend upon the coming space,
Expecting absent friends. As thou lovest her,
Thy love's to me religious; else, does err.

Exeunt all but LAFEU and PAROLLES

LAFEU
[Advancing] Do you hear, monsieur? a word with you.

PAROLLES
Your pleasure, sir?

LAFEU
Your lord and master did well to make his recantation.

PAROLLES
Recantation! My lord! my master!

LAFEU
Ay; is it not a language I speak?

PAROLLES
A most harsh one, and not to be understood without bloody succeeding. My master!

LAFEU
Are you companion to the Count Rousillon?

PAROLLES
To any count, to all counts, to what is man.

LAFEU
To what is count's man: count's master is of another style.

PAROLLES
You are too old, sir; let it satisfy you, you are too old.

LAFEU
I must tell thee, sirrah, I write man; to which title age cannot bring thee.

PAROLLES
What I dare too well do, I dare not do.

LAFEU
I did think thee, for two ordinaries, to be a pretty wise fellow; thou didst make tolerable vent of thy travel; it might pass: yet the scarfs and the bannerets about thee did manifoldly dissuade me from believing thee a vessel of too great a burthen. I have now found thee; when I lose thee again, I care not: yet art thou good for nothing but taking up; and that thou't scarce worth.

PAROLLES
Hadst thou not the privilege of antiquity upon thee,—

LAFEU
Do not plunge thyself too far in anger, lest thou hasten thy trial; which if—Lord have mercy on thee for a hen! So, my good window of lattice, fare thee well: thy casement I need not open, for I look through thee. Give me thy hand.

PAROLLES
My lord, you give me most egregious indignity.

LAFEU
Ay, with all my heart; and thou art worthy of it.

PAROLLES
I have not, my lord, deserved it.

LAFEU
Yes, good faith, every dram of it; and I will not bate thee a scruple.

PAROLLES
Well, I shall be wiser.

LAFEU
Even as soon as thou canst, for thou hast to pull at a smack o' the contrary. If ever thou be'st bound in thy scarf and beaten, thou shalt find what it is to be proud of thy bondage. I have a desire to hold

my acquaintance with thee, or rather my knowledge, that I may say in the default, he is a man I know.

PAROLLES
My lord, you do me most insupportable vexation.

LAFEU
I would it were hell-pains for thy sake, and my poor doing eternal: for doing I am past: as I will by thee, in what motion age will give me leave.

Exit

PAROLLES
Well, thou hast a son shall take this disgrace off me; scurvy, old, filthy, scurvy lord! Well, I must be patient; there is no fettering of authority. I'll beat him, by my life, if I can meet him with any convenience, an he were double and double a lord. I'll have no more pity of his age than I would of— I'll beat him, an if I could but meet him again.

Re-enter LAFEU

LAFEU
Sirrah, your lord and master's married; there's news
for you: you have a new mistress.

PAROLLES
I most unfeignedly beseech your lordship to make some reservation of your wrongs: he is my good lord: whom I serve above is my master.

LAFEU
Who? God?

PAROLLES
Ay, sir.

LAFEU
The devil it is that's thy master. Why dost thou garter up thy arms o' this fashion? dost make hose of sleeves? do other servants so? Thou wert best set thy lower part where thy nose stands. By mine honour, if I were but two hours younger, I'd beat thee: methinks, thou art a general offence, and every man should beat thee: I think thou wast created for men to breathe themselves upon thee.

PAROLLES
This is hard and undeserved measure, my lord.

LAFEU
Go to, sir; you were beaten in Italy for picking a kernel out of a pomegranate; you are a vagabond and no true traveller: you are more saucy with lords and honourable personages than the commission of your birth and virtue gives you heraldry. You are not worth another word, else I'd call you knave. I leave you.

Exit

PAROLLES
Good, very good; it is so then: good, very good; let it be concealed awhile.

Re-enter BERTRAM

BERTRAM
Undone, and forfeited to cares for ever!

PAROLLES
What's the matter, sweet-heart?

BERTRAM
Although before the solemn priest I have sworn,
I will not bed her.

PAROLLES
What, what, sweet-heart?

BERTRAM
O my Parolles, they have married me!
I'll to the Tuscan wars, and never bed her.

PAROLLES
France is a dog-hole, and it no more merits
The tread of a man's foot: to the wars!

BERTRAM
There's letters from my mother: what the import is,
I know not yet.

PAROLLES
Ay, that would be known. To the wars, my boy, to the wars!
He wears his honour in a box unseen,
That hugs his kicky-wicky here at home,
Spending his manly marrow in her arms,
Which should sustain the bound and high curvet
Of Mars's fiery steed. To other regions
France is a stable; we that dwell in't jades;
Therefore, to the war!

BERTRAM
It shall be so: I'll send her to my house,
Acquaint my mother with my hate to her,
And wherefore I am fled; write to the king
That which I durst not speak; his present gift
Shall furnish me to those Italian fields,
Where noble fellows strike: war is no strife
To the dark house and the detested wife.

PAROLLES
Will this capriccio hold in thee? art sure?

BERTRAM
Go with me to my chamber, and advise me.
I'll send her straight away: to-morrow
I'll to the wars, she to her single sorrow.

PAROLLES
Why, these balls bound; there's noise in it. 'Tis hard:
A young man married is a man that's marr'd:
Therefore away, and leave her bravely; go:
The king has done you wrong: but, hush, 'tis so.

Exeunt

SCENE IV. Paris. The King's Palace.

Enter HELENA and CLOWN

HELENA
My mother greets me kindly; is she well?

CLOWN
She is not well; but yet she has her health: she's very merry; but yet she is not well: but thanks be given, she's very well and wants nothing i', the world; but yet she is not well.

HELENA
If she be very well, what does she ail, that she's not very well?

CLOWN
Truly, she's very well indeed, but for two things.

HELENA
What two things?

CLOWN
One, that she's not in heaven, whither God send her quickly! the other that she's in earth, from whence God send her quickly!

Enter PAROLLES

PAROLLES
Bless you, my fortunate lady!

HELENA
I hope, sir, I have your good will to have mine own good fortunes.

PAROLLES
You had my prayers to lead them on; and to keep them on, have them still. O, my knave, how does my old lady?

Clown
So that you had her wrinkles and I her money,
I would she did as you say.

PAROLLES
Why, I say nothing.

CLOWN
Marry, you are the wiser man; for many a man's tongue shakes out his master's undoing: to say nothing, to do nothing, to know nothing, and to have nothing, is to be a great part of your title; which is within a very little of nothing.

PAROLLES
Away! thou'rt a knave.

CLOWN
You should have said, sir, before a knave thou'rt a knave; that's, before me thou'rt a knave: this had been truth, sir.

PAROLLES
Go to, thou art a witty fool; I have found thee.

CLOWN
Did you find me in yourself, sir? or were you taught to find me? The search, sir, was profitable; and much fool may you find in you, even to the world's pleasure and the increase of laughter.

PAROLLES
A good knave, i' faith, and well fed.
Madam, my lord will go away to-night;
A very serious business calls on him.
The great prerogative and rite of love,
Which, as your due, time claims, he does acknowledge;
But puts it off to a compell'd restraint;
Whose want, and whose delay, is strew'd with sweets,
Which they distil now in the curbed time,
To make the coming hour o'erflow with joy
And pleasure drown the brim.

HELENA
What's his will else?

PAROLLES
That you will take your instant leave o' the king
And make this haste as your own good proceeding,
Strengthen'd with what apology you think
May make it probable need.

HELENA
What more commands he?

PAROLLES
That, having this obtain'd, you presently
Attend his further pleasure.

HELENA
In every thing I wait upon his will.

PAROLLES
I shall report it so.

HELENA
I pray you.

Exit PAROLLES

Come, sirrah.

Exeunt

SCENE V. Paris. The King's Palace.

Enter LAFEU and BERTRAM

LAFEU
But I hope your lordship thinks not him a soldier.

BERTRAM
Yes, my lord, and of very valiant approof.

LAFEU
You have it from his own deliverance.

BERTRAM
And by other warranted testimony.

LAFEU
Then my dial goes not true: I took this lark for a bunting.

BERTRAM
I do assure you, my lord, he is very great in knowledge and accordingly valiant.

LAFEU
I have then sinned against his experience and transgressed against his valour; and my state that way is dangerous, since I cannot yet find in my heart to repent. Here he comes: I pray you, make us friends; I will pursue the amity.

Enter PAROLLES

PAROLLES

[To BERTRAM] These things shall be done, sir.

LAFEU
Pray you, sir, who's his tailor?

PAROLLES
Sir?

LAFEU
O, I know him well, I, sir; he, sir, 's a good workman, a very good tailor.

BERTRAM
[Aside to PAROLLES] Is she gone to the king?

PAROLLES
She is.

BERTRAM
Will she away to-night?

PAROLLES
As you'll have her.

BERTRAM
I have writ my letters, casketed my treasure,
Given order for our horses; and to-night,
When I should take possession of the bride,
End ere I do begin.

LAFEU
A good traveller is something at the latter end of a dinner; but one that lies three thirds and uses a known truth to pass a thousand nothings with, should be once heard and thrice beaten. God save you, captain.

BERTRAM
Is there any unkindness between my lord and you, monsieur?

PAROLLES
I know not how I have deserved to run into my lord's displeasure.

LAFEU
You have made shift to run into 't, boots and spurs and all, like him that leaped into the custard; and out of it you'll run again, rather than suffer question for your residence.

BERTRAM
It may be you have mistaken him, my lord.

LAFEU
And shall do so ever, though I took him at 's prayers. Fare you well, my lord; and believe this of me, there can be no kernel in this light nut; the soul of this man is his clothes. Trust him not in matter of heavy consequence; I have kept of them tame, and know their natures. Farewell,

monsieur: I have spoken better of you than you have or will to deserve at my hand; but we must do good against evil.

Exit

PAROLLES
An idle lord, I swear.

BERTRAM
I think so.

PAROLLES
Why, do you not know him?

BERTRAM
Yes, I do know him well, and common speech
Gives him a worthy pass. Here comes my clog.

Enter HELENA

HELENA
I have, sir, as I was commanded from you,
Spoke with the king and have procured his leave
For present parting; only he desires
Some private speech with you.

BERTRAM
I shall obey his will.
You must not marvel, Helen, at my course,
Which holds not colour with the time, nor does
The ministration and required office
On my particular. Prepared I was not
For such a business; therefore am I found
So much unsettled: this drives me to entreat you
That presently you take our way for home;
And rather muse than ask why I entreat you,
For my respects are better than they seem
And my appointments have in them a need
Greater than shows itself at the first view
To you that know them not. This to my mother:

Giving a letter

'Twill be two days ere I shall see you, so
I leave you to your wisdom.

HELENA
Sir, I can nothing say,
But that I am your most obedient servant.

BERTRAM

Come, come, no more of that.

HELENA
And ever shall
With true observance seek to eke out that
Wherein toward me my homely stars have fail'd
To equal my great fortune.

BERTRAM
Let that go:
My haste is very great: farewell; hie home.

HELENA
Pray, sir, your pardon.

BERTRAM
Well, what would you say?

HELENA
I am not worthy of the wealth I owe,
Nor dare I say 'tis mine, and yet it is;
But, like a timorous thief, most fain would steal
What law does vouch mine own.

BERTRAM
What would you have?

HELENA
Something; and scarce so much: nothing, indeed.
I would not tell you what I would, my lord:
Faith yes;
Strangers and foes do sunder, and not kiss.

BERTRAM
I pray you, stay not, but in haste to horse.
HELENA
I shall not break your bidding, good my lord.

BERTRAM
Where are my other men, monsieur? Farewell.

Exit HELENA

Go thou toward home; where I will never come
Whilst I can shake my sword or hear the drum.
Away, and for our flight.

PAROLLES
Bravely, coragio!

Exeunt

ACT III

SCENE I. Florence. The Duke's Palace.

Flourish. Enter the DUKE of Florence attended; the two Frenchmen, with a troop of soldiers.

DUKE
So that from point to point now have you heard
The fundamental reasons of this war,
Whose great decision hath much blood let forth
And more thirsts after.

FIRST LORD
Holy seems the quarrel
Upon your grace's part; black and fearful
On the opposer.

DUKE
Therefore we marvel much our cousin France
Would in so just a business shut his bosom
Against our borrowing prayers.

Second Lord
Good my lord,
The reasons of our state I cannot yield,
But like a common and an outward man,
That the great figure of a council frames
By self-unable motion: therefore dare not
Say what I think of it, since I have found
Myself in my incertain grounds to fail
As often as I guess'd.

DUKE
Be it his pleasure.

FIRST LORD
But I am sure the younger of our nature,
That surfeit on their ease, will day by day
Come here for physic.

DUKE
Welcome shall they be;
And all the honours that can fly from us
Shall on them settle. You know your places well;
When better fall, for your avails they fell:
To-morrow to the field.

Flourish. Exeunt

SCENE II. Rousillon. The Count's Palace.

Enter COUNTESS and CLOWN

COUNTESS
It hath happened all as I would have had it, save that he comes not along with her.

Clown
By my troth, I take my young lord to be a very melancholy man.

COUNTESS
By what observance, I pray you?

CLOWN
Why, he will look upon his boot and sing; mend the ruff and sing; ask questions and sing; pick his teeth and sing. I know a man that had this trick of melancholy sold a goodly manor for a song.

COUNTESS
Let me see what he writes, and when he means to come.

Opening a letter

CLOWN
I have no mind to Isbel since I was at court: our old ling and our Isbels o' the country are nothing like your old ling and your Isbels o' the court: the brains of my Cupid's knocked out, and I begin to love, as an old man loves money, with no stomach.

COUNTESS
What have we here?

CLOWN
E'en that you have there.

Exit

COUNTESS
[Reads] I have sent you a daughter-in-law: she hath
recovered the king, and undone me. I have wedded
her, not bedded her; and sworn to make the 'not'
eternal. You shall hear I am run away: know it
before the report come. If there be breadth enough
in the world, I will hold a long distance. My duty
to you. Your unfortunate son,
BERTRAM.
This is not well, rash and unbridled boy.
To fly the favours of so good a king;
To pluck his indignation on thy head

By the misprising of a maid too virtuous
For the contempt of empire.

Re-enter CLOWN

CLOWN
O madam, yonder is heavy news within between two soldiers and my young lady!

COUNTESS
What is the matter?

CLOWN
Nay, there is some comfort in the news, some comfort; your son will not be killed so soon as I thought he would.

COUNTESS
Why should he be killed?

CLOWN
So say I, madam, if he run away, as I hear he does: the danger is in standing to't; that's the loss of men, though it be the getting of children. Here they come will tell you more: for my part, I only hear your son was run away.

Exit

Enter HELENA, and two GENTLEMEN

FIRST GENTLEMAN
Save you, good madam.

HELENA
Madam, my lord is gone, for ever gone.

SECOND GENTLEMEN
Do not say so.

COUNTESS
Think upon patience. Pray you, gentlemen,
I have felt so many quirks of joy and grief,
That the first face of neither, on the start,
Can woman me unto't: where is my son, I pray you?

SECOND GENTLEMEN
Madam, he's gone to serve the duke of Florence:
We met him thitherward; for thence we came,
And, after some dispatch in hand at court,
Thither we bend again.

HELENA

Look on his letter, madam; here's my passport.
Reads
When thou canst get the ring upon my finger which never shall come off, and show me a child begotten of thy body that I am father to, then call me husband: but in such a 'then' I write a 'never.'
This is a dreadful sentence.

COUNTESS
Brought you this letter, gentlemen?

FIRST GENTLEMAN
Ay, madam;
And for the contents' sake are sorry for our pain.

COUNTESS
I prithee, lady, have a better cheer;
If thou engrossest all the griefs are thine,
Thou robb'st me of a moiety: he was my son;
But I do wash his name out of my blood,
And thou art all my child. Towards Florence is he?

SECOND GENTLEMAN
Ay, madam.

COUNTESS
And to be a soldier?

SECOND GENTLEMAN
Such is his noble purpose; and believe 't,
The duke will lay upon him all the honour
That good convenience claims.

COUNTESS
Return you thither?

FIRST GENTLEMAN
Ay, madam, with the swiftest wing of speed.

HELENA
[Reads] Till I have no wife I have nothing in France.
'Tis bitter.

COUNTESS
Find you that there?

HELENA
Ay, madam.

FIRST GENTLEMAN
'Tis but the boldness of his hand, haply, which his heart was not consenting to.

COUNTESS

Nothing in France, until he have no wife!
There's nothing here that is too good for him
But only she; and she deserves a lord
That twenty such rude boys might tend upon
And call her hourly mistress. Who was with him?

FIRST GENTLEMAN
A servant only, and a gentleman
Which I have sometime known.

COUNTESS
Parolles, was it not?

FIRST GENTLEMAN
Ay, my good lady, he.

COUNTESS
A very tainted fellow, and full of wickedness.
My son corrupts a well-derived nature
With his inducement.

FIRST GENTLEMAN
Indeed, good lady,
The fellow has a deal of that too much,
Which holds him much to have.

COUNTESS
You're welcome, gentlemen.
I will entreat you, when you see my son,
To tell him that his sword can never win
The honour that he loses: more I'll entreat you
Written to bear along.

SECOND GENTLEMAN
We serve you, madam,
In that and all your worthiest affairs.

COUNTESS
Not so, but as we change our courtesies.
Will you draw near!

Exeunt COUNTESS and GENTLEMEN

HELENA
'Till I have no wife, I have nothing in France.'
Nothing in France, until he has no wife!
Thou shalt have none, Rousillon, none in France;
Then hast thou all again. Poor lord! is't I
That chase thee from thy country and expose
Those tender limbs of thine to the event
Of the none-sparing war? and is it I

That drive thee from the sportive court, where thou
Wast shot at with fair eyes, to be the mark
Of smoky muskets? O you leaden messengers,
That ride upon the violent speed of fire,
Fly with false aim; move the still-peering air,
That sings with piercing; do not touch my lord.
Whoever shoots at him, I set him there;
Whoever charges on his forward breast,
I am the caitiff that do hold him to't;
And, though I kill him not, I am the cause
His death was so effected: better 'twere
I met the ravin lion when he roar'd
With sharp constraint of hunger; better 'twere
That all the miseries which nature owes
Were mine at once. No, come thou home, Rousillon,
Whence honour but of danger wins a scar,
As oft it loses all: I will be gone;
My being here it is that holds thee hence:
Shall I stay here to do't? no, no, although
The air of paradise did fan the house
And angels officed all: I will be gone,
That pitiful rumour may report my flight,
To consolate thine ear. Come, night; end, day!
For with the dark, poor thief, I'll steal away.

Exit

SCENE III. Florence. Before the Duke's Palace.

Flourish. Enter the DUKE of Florence, BERTRAM, PAROLLES, Soldiers, Drum, and Trumpets

DUKE
The general of our horse thou art; and we,
Great in our hope, lay our best love and credence
Upon thy promising fortune.

BERTRAM
Sir, it is
A charge too heavy for my strength, but yet
We'll strive to bear it for your worthy sake
To the extreme edge of hazard.

DUKE
Then go thou forth;
And fortune play upon thy prosperous helm,
As thy auspicious mistress!

BERTRAM

This very day,
Great Mars, I put myself into thy file:
Make me but like my thoughts, and I shall prove
A lover of thy drum, hater of love.

Exeunt

SCENE IV. Rousillon. The Count's Palace.

Enter COUNTESS and STEWARD

COUNTESS
Alas! and would you take the letter of her?
Might you not know she would do as she has done,
By sending me a letter? Read it again.

STEWARD
[Reads]
I am Saint Jaques' pilgrim, thither gone:
Ambitious love hath so in me offended,
That barefoot plod I the cold ground upon,
With sainted vow my faults to have amended.
Write, write, that from the bloody course of war
My dearest master, your dear son, may hie:
Bless him at home in peace, whilst I from far
His name with zealous fervor sanctify:
His taken labours bid him me forgive;
I, his despiteful Juno, sent him forth
From courtly friends, with camping foes to live,
Where death and danger dogs the heels of worth:
He is too good and fair for death and me:
Whom I myself embrace, to set him free.

COUNTESS
Ah, what sharp stings are in her mildest words!
Rinaldo, you did never lack advice so much,
As letting her pass so: had I spoke with her,
I could have well diverted her intents,
Which thus she hath prevented.

STEWARD
Pardon me, madam:
If I had given you this at over-night,
She might have been o'erta'en; and yet she writes,
Pursuit would be but vain.

COUNTESS
What angel shall
Bless this unworthy husband? he cannot thrive,

Unless her prayers, whom heaven delights to hear
And loves to grant, reprieve him from the wrath
Of greatest justice. Write, write, Rinaldo,
To this unworthy husband of his wife;
Let every word weigh heavy of her worth
That he does weigh too light: my greatest grief.
Though little he do feel it, set down sharply.
Dispatch the most convenient messenger:
When haply he shall hear that she is gone,
He will return; and hope I may that she,
Hearing so much, will speed her foot again,
Led hither by pure love: which of them both
Is dearest to me. I have no skill in sense
To make distinction: provide this messenger:
My heart is heavy and mine age is weak;
Grief would have tears, and sorrow bids me speak.

Exeunt

SCENE V. Florence. Without the Walls. A Tucket Afar Off.

Enter an old WIDOW of Florence, DIANA, VIOLENTA, and MARIANA, with other Citizens

WIDOW
Nay, come; for if they do approach the city, we shall lose all the sight.

DIANA
They say the French count has done most honourable service.

WIDOW
It is reported that he has taken their greatest commander; and that with his own hand he slew the duke's brother.

Tucket

We have lost our labour; they are gone a contrary way: hark! you may know by their trumpets.

MARIANA
Come, let's return again, and suffice ourselves with the report of it. Well, Diana, take heed of this French earl: the honour of a maid is her name; and no legacy is so rich as honesty.

WIDOW
I have told my neighbour how you have been solicited by a gentleman his companion.

MARIANA
I know that knave; hang him! one Parolles: a filthy officer he is in those suggestions for the young earl. Beware of them, Diana; their promises, enticements, oaths, tokens, and all these engines of lust, are not the things they go under: many a maid hath been seduced by them; and the misery is, example, that so terrible shows in the wreck of maidenhood, cannot for all that dissuade succession,

but that they are limed with the twigs that threaten them. I hope I need not to advise you further; but I hope your own grace will keep you where you are, though there were no further danger known but the modesty which is so lost.

DIANA
You shall not need to fear me.

WIDOW
I hope so.

Enter HELENA, disguised like a Pilgrim

Look, here comes a pilgrim: I know she will lie at my house; thither they send one another: I'll question her. God save you, pilgrim! whither are you bound?

HELENA
To Saint Jaques le Grand.
Where do the palmers lodge, I do beseech you?

WIDOW
At the Saint Francis here beside the port.

HELENA
Is this the way?

WIDOW
Ay, marry, is't.
A march afar
Hark you! they come this way.
If you will tarry, holy pilgrim,
But till the troops come by,
I will conduct you where you shall be lodged;
The rather, for I think I know your hostess
As ample as myself.

HELENA
Is it yourself?

WIDOW
If you shall please so, pilgrim.

HELENA
I thank you, and will stay upon your leisure.

WIDOW
You came, I think, from France?

HELENA
I did so.

WIDOW

Here you shall see a countryman of yours
That has done worthy service.

HELENA
His name, I pray you.

DIANA
The Count Rousillon: know you such a one?

HELENA
But by the ear, that hears most nobly of him:
His face I know not.

DIANA
Whatsome'er he is,
He's bravely taken here. He stole from France,
As 'tis reported, for the king had married him
Against his liking: think you it is so?

HELENA
Ay, surely, mere the truth: I know his lady.

DIANA
There is a gentleman that serves the count
Reports but coarsely of her.

HELENA
What's his name?

DIANA
Monsieur Parolles.

HELENA
O, I believe with him,
In argument of praise, or to the worth
Of the great count himself, she is too mean
To have her name repeated: all her deserving
Is a reserved honesty, and that
I have not heard examined.

DIANA
Alas, poor lady!
'Tis a hard bondage to become the wife
Of a detesting lord.

Widow
I warrant, good creature, wheresoe'er she is,
Her heart weighs sadly: this young maid might do her
A shrewd turn, if she pleased.

HELENA

How do you mean?
May be the amorous count solicits her
In the unlawful purpose.

Widow
He does indeed;
And brokes with all that can in such a suit
Corrupt the tender honour of a maid:
But she is arm'd for him and keeps her guard
In honestest defence.

MARIANA
The gods forbid else!

Widow
So, now they come:

Drum and Colours

Enter BERTRAM, PAROLLES, and the whole army

That is Antonio, the duke's eldest son;
That, Escalus.

HELENA
Which is the Frenchman?

DIANA
He; That with the plume: 'tis a most gallant fellow.
I would he loved his wife: if he were honester
He were much goodlier: is't not a handsome gentleman?

HELENA
I like him well.

DIANA
'Tis pity he is not honest: yond's that same knave
That leads him to these places: were I his lady,
I would Poison that vile rascal.

HELENA
Which is he?

DIANA
That jack-an-apes with scarfs: why is he melancholy?

HELENA
Perchance he's hurt i' the battle.

PAROLLES
Lose our drum! well.

MARIANA
He's shrewdly vexed at something: look, he has spied us.

WIDOW
Marry, hang you!

MARIANA
And your courtesy, for a ring-carrier!

Exeunt BERTRAM, PAROLLES, and army

WIDOW
The troop is past. Come, pilgrim, I will bring you
Where you shall host: of enjoin'd penitents
There's four or five, to great Saint Jaques bound,
Already at my house.

HELENA
I humbly thank you:
Please it this matron and this gentle maid
To eat with us to-night, the charge and thanking
Shall be for me; and, to requite you further,
I will bestow some precepts of this virgin
Worthy the note.

BOTH
We'll take your offer kindly.

Exeunt

SCENE VI. Camp Before Florence.

Enter BERTRAM and the two French LORDS

SECOND LORD
Nay, good my lord, put him to't; let him have his way.

FIRST LORD
If your lordship find him not a hilding, hold me no more in your respect.

SECOND LORD
On my life, my lord, a bubble.

BERTRAM
Do you think I am so far deceived in him?

SECOND LORD

Believe it, my lord, in mine own direct knowledge, without any malice, but to speak of him as my kinsman, he's a most notable coward, an infinite and endless liar, an hourly promise-breaker, the owner of no one good quality worthy your lordship's entertainment.

FIRST LORD
It were fit you knew him; lest, reposing too far in his virtue, which he hath not, he might at some great and trusty business in a main danger fail you.

BERTRAM
I would I knew in what particular action to try him.

FIRST LORD
None better than to let him fetch off his drum, which you hear him so confidently undertake to do.

SECOND LORD
I, with a troop of Florentines, will suddenly surprise him; such I will have, whom I am sure he knows not from the enemy: we will bind and hoodwink him so, that he shall suppose no other but that he is carried into the leaguer of the adversaries, when we bring him to our own tents. Be but your lordship present at his examination: if he do not, for the promise of his life and in the highest compulsion of base fear, offer to betray you and deliver all the intelligence in his power against you, and that with the divine forfeit of his soul upon oath, never trust my judgment in any thing.

FIRST LORD
O, for the love of laughter, let him fetch his drum; he says he has a stratagem for't: when your lordship sees the bottom of his success in't, and to what metal this counterfeit lump of ore will be melted, if you give him not John Drum's entertainment, your inclining cannot be removed. Here he comes.

Enter PAROLLES

SECOND LORD
[Aside to BERTRAM] O, for the love of laughter, hinder not the honour of his design: let him fetch off his drum in any hand.

BERTRAM
How now, monsieur! this drum sticks sorely in your disposition.

FIRST LORD
A pox on't, let it go; 'tis but a drum.

PAROLLES
'But a drum'! is't 'but a drum'? A drum so lost! There was excellent command,—to charge in with our horse upon our own wings, and to rend our own soldiers!

FIRST LORD
That was not to be blamed in the command of the service: it was a disaster of war that Caesar himself could not have prevented, if he had been there to command.

BERTRAM
Well, we cannot greatly condemn our success: some dishonour we had in the loss of that drum; but it is not to be recovered.

PAROLLES
It might have been recovered.

BERTRAM
It might; but it is not now.

PAROLLES
It is to be recovered: but that the merit of service is seldom attributed to the true and exact performer, I would have that drum or another, or 'hic jacet.'

BERTRAM
Why, if you have a stomach, to't, monsieur: if you think your mystery in stratagem can bring this instrument of honour again into his native quarter, be magnanimous in the enterprise and go on; I will grace the attempt for a worthy exploit: if you speed well in it, the duke shall both speak of it. and extend to you what further becomes his greatness, even to the utmost syllable of your worthiness.

PAROLLES
By the hand of a soldier, I will undertake it.

BERTRAM
But you must not now slumber in it.

PAROLLES
I'll about it this evening: and I will presently pen down my dilemmas, encourage myself in my certainty, put myself into my mortal preparation; and by midnight look to hear further from me.

BERTRAM
May I be bold to acquaint his grace you are gone about it?

PAROLLES
I know not what the success will be, my lord; but the attempt I vow.

BERTRAM
I know thou'rt valiant; and, to the possibility of thy soldiership, will subscribe for thee. Farewell.

PAROLLES
I love not many words.

Exit

SECOND LORD
No more than a fish loves water. Is not this a strange fellow, my lord, that so confidently seems to undertake this business, which he knows is not to be done; damns himself to do and dares better be damned than to do't?

FIRST LORD
You do not know him, my lord, as we do: certain it is that he will steal himself into a man's favour and for a week escape a great deal of discoveries; but when you find him out, you have him ever after.

BERTRAM
Why, do you think he will make no deed at all of this that so seriously he does address himself unto?

SECOND LORD
None in the world; but return with an invention and clap upon you two or three probable lies: but we have almost embossed him; you shall see his fall to-night; for indeed he is not for your lordship's respect.

FIRST LORD
We'll make you some sport with the fox ere we case him. He was first smoked by the old lord Lafeu: when his disguise and he is parted, tell me what a sprat you shall find him; which you shall see this very night.

SECOND LORD
I must go look my twigs: he shall be caught.

BERTRAM
Your brother he shall go along with me.

SECOND LORD
As't please your lordship: I'll leave you.

Exit

BERTRAM
Now will I lead you to the house, and show you
The lass I spoke of.

FIRST LORD
But you say she's honest.

BERTRAM
That's all the fault: I spoke with her but once
And found her wondrous cold; but I sent to her,
By this same coxcomb that we have i' the wind,
Tokens and letters which she did re-send;
And this is all I have done. She's a fair creature:
Will you go see her?

FIRST LORD
With all my heart, my lord.

Exeunt

SCENE VII. Florence. The Widow's House.

Enter HELENA and WIDOW

HELENA
If you misdoubt me that I am not she,
I know not how I shall assure you further,
But I shall lose the grounds I work upon.

WIDOW
Though my estate be fallen, I was well born,
Nothing acquainted with these businesses;
And would not put my reputation now
In any staining act.

HELENA
Nor would I wish you.
First, give me trust, the count he is my husband,
And what to your sworn counsel I have spoken
Is so from word to word; and then you cannot,
By the good aid that I of you shall borrow,
Err in bestowing it.

WIDOW
I should believe you:
For you have show'd me that which well approves
You're great in fortune.

HELENA
Take this purse of gold,
And let me buy your friendly help thus far,
Which I will over-pay and pay again
When I have found it. The count he wooes your daughter,
Lays down his wanton siege before her beauty,
Resolved to carry her: let her in fine consent,
As we'll direct her how 'tis best to bear it.
Now his important blood will nought deny
That she'll demand: a ring the county wears,
That downward hath succeeded in his house
From son to son, some four or five descents
Since the first father wore it: this ring he holds
In most rich choice; yet in his idle fire,
To buy his will, it would not seem too dear,
Howe'er repented after.

WIDOW
Now I see
The bottom of your purpose.

HELENA
You see it lawful, then: it is no more,
But that your daughter, ere she seems as won,
Desires this ring; appoints him an encounter;
In fine, delivers me to fill the time,
Herself most chastely absent: after this,

To marry her, I'll add three thousand crowns
To what is passed already.

WIDOW
I have yielded:
Instruct my daughter how she shall persever,
That time and place with this deceit so lawful
May prove coherent. Every night he comes
With musics of all sorts and songs composed
To her unworthiness: it nothing steads us
To chide him from our eaves; for he persists
As if his life lay on't.

HELENA
Why then to-night
Let us assay our plot; which, if it speed,
Is wicked meaning in a lawful deed
And lawful meaning in a lawful act,
Where both not sin, and yet a sinful fact:
But let's about it.

Exeunt

ACT IV

SCENE I. Without the Florentine Camp.

Enter Second French LORD, with five or six other SOLDIERS in ambush

SECOND LORD
He can come no other way but by this hedge-corner. When you sally upon him, speak what terrible language you will: though you understand it not yourselves, no matter; for we must not seem to understand him, unless some one among us whom we must produce for an interpreter.

FIRST SOLDIER
Good captain, let me be the interpreter.

SECOND LORD
Art not acquainted with him? knows he not thy voice?

FIRST SOLDIER
No, sir, I warrant you.

SECOND LORD
But what linsey-woolsey hast thou to speak to us again?

FIRST SOLDIER
E'en such as you speak to me.

SECOND LORD
He must think us some band of strangers i' the adversary's entertainment. Now he hath a smack of all neighbouring languages; therefore we must every one be a man of his own fancy, not to know what we speak one to another; so we seem to know, is to know straight our purpose: choughs' language, gabble enough, and good enough. As for you, interpreter, you must seem very politic. But couch, ho! here he comes, to beguile two hours in a sleep, and then to return and swear the lies he forges.

Enter PAROLLES

PAROLLES
Ten o'clock: within these three hours 'twill be time enough to go home. What shall I say I have done? It must be a very plausive invention that carries it: they begin to smoke me; and disgraces have of late knocked too often at my door. I find my tongue is too foolhardy; but my heart hath the fear of Mars before it and of his creatures, not daring the reports of my tongue.

Second Lord
This is the first truth that e'er thine own tongue
was guilty of.

PAROLLES
What the devil should move me to undertake the recovery of this drum, being not ignorant of the impossibility, and knowing I had no such purpose? I must give myself some hurts, and say I got them in exploit: yet slight ones will not carry it; they will say, 'Came you off with so little?' and great ones I dare not give. Wherefore, what's the instance? Tongue, I must put you into a butter-woman's mouth and buy myself another of Bajazet's mule, if you prattle me into these perils.

SECOND LORD
Is it possible he should know what he is, and be that he is?

PAROLLES
I would the cutting of my garments would serve the turn, or the breaking of my Spanish sword.

SECOND LORD
We cannot afford you so.

PAROLLES
Or the baring of my beard; and to say it was in stratagem.

SECOND LORD
'Twould not do.

PAROLLES
Or to drown my clothes, and say I was stripped.

SECOND LORD
Hardly serve.

PAROLLES
Though I swore I leaped from the window of the citadel.

SECOND LORD
How deep?

PAROLLES
Thirty fathom.

SECOND LORD
Three great oaths would scarce make that be believed.

PAROLLES
I would I had any drum of the enemy's: I would swear
I recovered it.

SECOND LORD
You shall hear one anon.

PAROLLES
A drum now of the enemy's,—

Alarum within

SECOND LORD
Throca movousus, cargo, cargo, cargo.

ALL
Cargo, cargo, cargo, villiando par corbo, cargo.

PAROLLES
O, ransom, ransom! do not hide mine eyes.

They seize and blindfold him

FIRST SOLDIER
Boskos thromuldo boskos.

PAROLLES
I know you are the Muskos' regiment:
And I shall lose my life for want of language;
If there be here German, or Dane, low Dutch,
Italian, or French, let him speak to me; I'll
Discover that which shall undo the Florentine.

FIRST SOLDIER
Boskos vauvado: I understand thee, and can speak thy tongue. Kerely bonto, sir, betake thee to thy faith, for seventeen poniards are at thy bosom.

PAROLLES
O!

FIRST SOLDIER
O, pray, pray, pray! Manka revania dulche.

SECOND LORD
Oscorbidulchos volivorco.

FIRST SOLDIER
The general is content to spare thee yet;
And, hoodwink'd as thou art, will lead thee on
To gather from thee: haply thou mayst inform
Something to save thy life.

PAROLLES
O, let me live!
And all the secrets of our camp I'll show,
Their force, their purposes; nay, I'll speak that
Which you will wonder at.

FIRST SOLDIER
But wilt thou faithfully?

PAROLLES
If I do not, damn me.

FIRST SOLDIER
Acordo linta.
Come on; thou art granted space.

Exit, with PAROLLES guarded. A short alarum within

SECOND LORD
Go, tell the Count Rousillon, and my brother,
We have caught the woodcock, and will keep him muffled
Till we do hear from them.

SECOND SOLDIER
Captain, I will.

SECOND LORD
A' will betray us all unto ourselves:
Inform on that.

SECOND SOLDIER
So I will, sir.

SECOND LORD
Till then I'll keep him dark and safely lock'd.

Exeunt

SCENE II. Florence. The Widow's House.

Enter BERTRAM and DIANA

BERTRAM
They told me that your name was Fontibell.

DIANA
No, my good lord, Diana.

BERTRAM
Titled goddess;
And worth it, with addition! But, fair soul,
In your fine frame hath love no quality?
If quick fire of youth light not your mind,
You are no maiden, but a monument:
When you are dead, you should be such a one
As you are now, for you are cold and stem;
And now you should be as your mother was
When your sweet self was got.

DIANA
She then was honest.

BERTRAM
So should you be.

DIANA
No:
My mother did but duty; such, my lord,
As you owe to your wife.

BERTRAM
No more o' that;
I prithee, do not strive against my vows:
I was compell'd to her; but I love thee
By love's own sweet constraint, and will for ever
Do thee all rights of service.

DIANA
Ay, so you serve us
Till we serve you; but when you have our roses,
You barely leave our thorns to prick ourselves
And mock us with our bareness.

BERTRAM
How have I sworn!

DIANA
'Tis not the many oaths that makes the truth,
But the plain single vow that is vow'd true.
What is not holy, that we swear not by,

But take the High'st to witness: then, pray you, tell me,
If I should swear by God's great attributes,
I loved you dearly, would you believe my oaths,
When I did love you ill? This has no holding,
To swear by him whom I protest to love,
That I will work against him: therefore your oaths
Are words and poor conditions, but unseal'd,
At least in my opinion.

BERTRAM
Change it, change it;
Be not so holy-cruel: love is holy;
And my integrity ne'er knew the crafts
That you do charge men with. Stand no more off,
But give thyself unto my sick desires,
Who then recover: say thou art mine, and ever
My love as it begins shall so persever.

DIANA
I see that men make ropes in such a scarre
That we'll forsake ourselves. Give me that ring.

BERTRAM
I'll lend it thee, my dear; but have no power
To give it from me.

DIANA
Will you not, my lord?

BERTRAM
It is an honour 'longing to our house,
Bequeathed down from many ancestors;
Which were the greatest obloquy i' the world
In me to lose.

DIANA
Mine honour's such a ring:
My chastity's the jewel of our house,
Bequeathed down from many ancestors;
Which were the greatest obloquy i' the world
In me to lose: thus your own proper wisdom
Brings in the champion Honour on my part,
Against your vain assault.

BERTRAM
Here, take my ring:
My house, mine honour, yea, my life, be thine,
And I'll be bid by thee.

DIANA

When midnight comes, knock at my chamber-window:
I'll order take my mother shall not hear.
Now will I charge you in the band of truth,
When you have conquer'd my yet maiden bed,
Remain there but an hour, nor speak to me:
My reasons are most strong; and you shall know them
When back again this ring shall be deliver'd:
And on your finger in the night I'll put
Another ring, that what in time proceeds
May token to the future our past deeds.
Adieu, till then; then, fail not. You have won
A wife of me, though there my hope be done.

BERTRAM
A heaven on earth I have won by wooing thee.

Exit

DIANA
For which live long to thank both heaven and me!
You may so in the end.
My mother told me just how he would woo,
As if she sat in 's heart; she says all men
Have the like oaths: he had sworn to marry me
When his wife's dead; therefore I'll lie with him
When I am buried. Since Frenchmen are so braid,
Marry that will, I live and die a maid:
Only in this disguise I think't no sin
To cozen him that would unjustly win.

Exit

SCENE III. The Florentine Camp.

Enter the two French LORDS and some two or three SOLDIERS

FIRST LORD
You have not given him his mother's letter?

SECOND LORD
I have delivered it an hour since: there is something in't that stings his nature; for on the reading it he changed almost into another man.

FIRST LORD
He has much worthy blame laid upon him for shaking off so good a wife and so sweet a lady.

SECOND LORD
Especially he hath incurred the everlasting displeasure of the king, who had even tuned his bounty to sing happiness to him. I will tell you a thing, but you shall let it dwell darkly with you.

FIRST LORD
When you have spoken it, 'tis dead, and I am the grave of it.

SECOND LORD
He hath perverted a young gentlewoman here in Florence, of a most chaste renown; and this night he fleshes his will in the spoil of her honour: he hath given her his monumental ring, and thinks himself made in the unchaste composition.

FIRST LORD
Now, God delay our rebellion! as we are ourselves, what things are we!

SECOND LORD
Merely our own traitors. And as in the common course of all treasons, we still see them reveal themselves, till they attain to their abhorred ends, so he that in this action contrives against his own nobility, in his proper stream o'erflows himself.

FIRST LORD
Is it not meant damnable in us, to be trumpeters of our unlawful intents? We shall not then have his company to-night?

SECOND LORD
Not till after midnight; for he is dieted to his hour.

FIRST LORD
That approaches apace; I would gladly have him see his company anatomized, that he might take a measure of his own judgments, wherein so curiously he had set this counterfeit.

SECOND LORD
We will not meddle with him till he come; for his presence must be the whip of the other.

FIRST LORD
In the mean time, what hear you of these wars?

SECOND LORD
I hear there is an overture of peace.

FIRST LORD
Nay, I assure you, a peace concluded.

SECOND LORD
What will Count Rousillon do then? will he travel higher, or return again into France?

FIRST LORD
I perceive, by this demand, you are not altogether of his council.

SECOND LORD
Let it be forbid, sir; so should I be a great deal of his act.

FIRST LORD

Sir, his wife some two months since fled from his house: her pretence is a pilgrimage to Saint Jaques le Grand; which holy undertaking with most austere sanctimony she accomplished; and, there residing the tenderness of her nature became as a prey to her grief; in fine, made a groan of her last breath, and now she sings in heaven.

SECOND LORD
How is this justified?

FIRST LORD
The stronger part of it by her own letters, which makes her story true, even to the point of her death: her death itself, which could not be her office to say is come, was faithfully confirmed by the rector of the place.

SECOND LORD
Hath the count all this intelligence?

FIRST LORD
Ay, and the particular confirmations, point from point, so to the full arming of the verity.

SECOND LORD
I am heartily sorry that he'll be glad of this.

FIRST LORD
How mightily sometimes we make us comforts of our losses!

SECOND LORD
And how mightily some other times we drown our gain in tears! The great dignity that his valour hath here acquired for him shall at home be encountered with a shame as ample.

FIRST LORD
The web of our life is of a mingled yarn, good and ill together: our virtues would be proud, if our faults whipped them not; and our crimes would despair, if they were not cherished by our virtues.

Enter a MESSENGER

How now! where's your master?

SERVANT
He met the duke in the street, sir, of whom he hath taken a solemn leave: his lordship will next morning for France. The duke hath offered him letters of commendations to the king.

SECOND LORD
They shall be no more than needful there, if they were more than they can commend.

FIRST LORD
They cannot be too sweet for the king's tartness.
Here's his lordship now.

Enter BERTRAM

How now, my lord! is't not after midnight?

BERTRAM
I have to-night dispatched sixteen businesses, a month's length a-piece, by an abstract of success: I have congied with the duke, done my adieu with his nearest; buried a wife, mourned for her; writ to my lady mother I am returning; entertained my convoy; and between these main parcels of dispatch effected many nicer needs; the last was the greatest, but that I have not ended yet.

SECOND LORD
If the business be of any difficulty, and this morning your departure hence, it requires haste of your lordship.

BERTRAM
I mean, the business is not ended, as fearing to hear of it hereafter. But shall we have this dialogue between the fool and the soldier? Come, bring forth this counterfeit module, he has deceived me, like a double-meaning prophesier.

SECOND LORD
Bring him forth: has sat i' the stocks all night, poor gallant knave.

BERTRAM
No matter: his heels have deserved it, in usurping his spurs so long. How does he carry himself?

SECOND LORD
I have told your lordship already, the stocks carry him. But to answer you as you would be understood; he weeps like a wench that had shed her milk: he hath confessed himself to Morgan, whom he supposes to be a friar, from the time of his remembrance to this very instant disaster of his setting i' the stocks: and what think you he hath confessed?

BERTRAM
Nothing of me, has a'?

SECOND LORD
His confession is taken, and it shall be read to his face: if your lordship be in't, as I believe you are, you must have the patience to hear it.

Enter PAROLLES guarded, and FIRST SOLDIER

BERTRAM
A plague upon him! muffled! he can say nothing of me: hush, hush!

FIRST LORD
Hoodman comes! Portotartarosa

FIRST SOLDIER
He calls for the tortures: what will you say without 'em?

PAROLLES
I will confess what I know without constraint: if ye pinch me like a pasty, I can say no more.

FIRST SOLDIER
Bosko chimurcho.

FIRST LORD
Boblibindo chicurmurco.

FIRST SOLDIER
You are a merciful general. Our general bids you answer to what I shall ask you out of a note.

PAROLLES
And truly, as I hope to live.

FIRST SOLDIER
[Reads] 'First demand of him how many horse the duke is strong.' What say you to that?

PAROLLES
Five or six thousand; but very weak and unserviceable: the troops are all scattered, and the commanders very poor rogues, upon my reputation and credit and as I hope to live.

FIRST SOLDIER
Shall I set down your answer so?

PAROLLES
Do: I'll take the sacrament on't, how and which way you will.

BERTRAM
All's one to him. What a past-saving slave is this!

FIRST LORD
You're deceived, my lord: this is Monsieur Parolles, the gallant militarist,—that was his own phrase,—that had the whole theoric of war in the knot of his scarf, and the practise in the chape of his dagger.

SECOND LORD
I will never trust a man again for keeping his sword clean. nor believe he can have every thing in him by wearing his apparel neatly.

FIRST SOLDIER
Well, that's set down.

PAROLLES
Five or six thousand horse, I said,— I will say true,—or thereabouts, set down, for I'll speak truth.

FIRST LORD
He's very near the truth in this.

BERTRAM
But I con him no thanks for't, in the nature he delivers it.

PAROLLES
Poor rogues, I pray you, say.

FIRST SOLDIER

Well, that's set down.

PAROLLES
I humbly thank you, sir: a truth's a truth, the rogues are marvellous poor.

FIRST SOLDIER
[Reads] 'Demand of him, of what strength they are a-foot.' What say you to that?

PAROLLES
By my troth, sir, if I were to live this present hour, I will tell true. Let me see: Spurio, a hundred and fifty; Sebastian, so many; Corambus, so many; Jaques, so many; Guiltian, Cosmo, Lodowick, and Gratii, two hundred and fifty each; mine own company, Chitopher, Vaumond, Bentii, two hundred and fifty each: so that the muster-file, rotten and sound, upon my life, amounts not to fifteen thousand poll; half of the which dare not shake snow from off their cassocks, lest they shake themselves to pieces.

BERTRAM
What shall be done to him?

FIRST LORD
Nothing, but let him have thanks. Demand of him my condition, and what credit I have with the duke.

FIRST SOLDIER
Well, that's set down.

Reads

'You shall demand of him, whether one Captain Dumain be i' the camp, a Frenchman; what his reputation is with the duke; what his valour, honesty, and expertness in wars; or whether he thinks it were not possible, with well-weighing sums of gold, to corrupt him to revolt.' What say you to this? What do you know of it?

PAROLLES
I beseech you, let me answer to the particular of the inter'gatories: demand them singly.

FIRST SOLDIER
Do you know this Captain Dumain?

PAROLLES
I know him: a' was a botcher's 'prentice in Paris, from whence he was whipped for getting the shrieve's fool with child,—a dumb innocent, that could not say him nay.

BERTRAM
Nay, by your leave, hold your hands; though I know his brains are forfeit to the next tile that falls.

FIRST SOLDIER
Well, is this captain in the duke of Florence's camp?

PAROLLES
Upon my knowledge, he is, and lousy.

FIRST LORD
Nay look not so upon me; we shall hear of your lordship anon.

FIRST SOLDIER
What is his reputation with the duke?

PAROLLES
The duke knows him for no other but a poor officer of mine; and writ to me this other day to turn him out o' the band: I think I have his letter in my pocket.

FIRST SOLDIER
Marry, we'll search.

PAROLLES
In good sadness, I do not know; either it is there, or it is upon a file with the duke's other letters in my tent.

FIRST SOLDIER
Here 'tis; here's a paper: shall I read it to you?

PAROLLES
I do not know if it be it or no.

BERTRAM
Our interpreter does it well.

FIRST LORD
Excellently.

FIRST SOLDIER
 [Reads] 'Dian, the count's a fool, and full of gold,'—

PAROLLES
That is not the duke's letter, sir; that is an advertisement to a proper maid in Florence, one Diana, to take heed of the allurement of one Count Rousillon, a foolish idle boy, but for all that very ruttish: I pray you, sir, put it up again.

FIRST SOLDIER
Nay, I'll read it first, by your favour.

PAROLLES
My meaning in't, I protest, was very honest in the behalf of the maid; for I knew the young count to be a dangerous and lascivious boy, who is a whale to virginity and devours up all the fry it finds.

BERTRAM
Damnable both-sides rogue!

FIRST SOLDIER
 [Reads] 'When he swears oaths, bid him drop gold, and take it;
After he scores, he never pays the score:

Half won is match well made; match, and well make it;
He ne'er pays after-debts, take it before;
And say a soldier, Dian, told thee this,
Men are to mell with, boys are not to kiss:
For count of this, the count's a fool, I know it,
Who pays before, but not when he does owe it.
Thine, as he vowed to thee in thine ear,
PAROLLES.'

BERTRAM
He shall be whipped through the army with this rhyme in's forehead.

SECOND LORD
This is your devoted friend, sir, the manifold linguist and the armipotent soldier.

BERTRAM
I could endure any thing before but a cat, and now he's a cat to me.

FIRST SOLDIER
I perceive, sir, by the general's looks, we shall be fain to hang you.

PAROLLES
My life, sir, in any case: not that I am afraid to die; but that, my offences being many, I would repent out the remainder of nature: let me live, sir, in a dungeon, i' the stocks, or any where, so I may live.

FIRST SOLDIER
We'll see what may be done, so you confess freely; therefore, once more to this Captain Dumain: you have answered to his reputation with the duke and to his valour: what is his honesty?

PAROLLES
He will steal, sir, an egg out of a cloister: for rapes and ravishments he parallels Nessus: he professes not keeping of oaths; in breaking 'em he is stronger than Hercules: he will lie, sir, with such volubility, that you would think truth were a fool: drunkenness is his best virtue, for he will be swine-drunk; and in his sleep he does little harm, save to his bed-clothes about him; but they know his conditions and lay him in straw. I have but little more to say, sir, of his honesty: he has every thing that an honest man should not have; what an honest man should have, he has nothing.

FIRST LORD
I begin to love him for this.

BERTRAM
For this description of thine honesty? A pox upon him for me, he's more and more a cat.

FIRST SOLDIER
What say you to his expertness in war?

PAROLLES
Faith, sir, he has led the drum before the English tragedians; to belie him, I will not, and more of his soldiership I know not; except, in that country he had the honour to be the officer at a place there called Mile-end, to instruct for the doubling of files: I would do the man what honour I can, but of this I am not certain.

FIRST LORD
He hath out-villained villany so far, that the rarity redeems him.

BERTRAM
A pox on him, he's a cat still.

FIRST SOLDIER
His qualities being at this poor price, I need not to ask you if gold will corrupt him to revolt.

PAROLLES
Sir, for a quart d'ecu he will sell the fee-simple of his salvation, the inheritance of it; and cut the entail from all remainders, and a perpetual succession for it perpetually.

FIRST SOLDIER
What's his brother, the other Captain Dumain?

SECOND LORD
Why does be ask him of me?

FIRST SOLDIER
What's he?

PAROLLES
E'en a crow o' the same nest; not altogether so great as the first in goodness, but greater a great deal in evil: he excels his brother for a coward, yet his brother is reputed one of the best that is: in a retreat he outruns any lackey; marry, in coming on he has the cramp.

FIRST SOLDIER
If your life be saved, will you undertake to betray the Florentine?

PAROLLES
Ay, and the captain of his horse, Count Rousillon.

FIRST SOLDIER
I'll whisper with the general, and know his pleasure.

PAROLLES
[Aside] I'll no more drumming; a plague of all drums! Only to seem to deserve well, and to beguile the supposition of that lascivious young boy the count, have I run into this danger. Yet who would have suspected an ambush where I was taken?

FIRST SOLDIER
There is no remedy, sir, but you must die: the general says, you that have so traitorously discovered the secrets of your army and made such pestiferous reports of men very nobly held, can serve the world for no honest use; therefore you must die. Come, headsman, off with his head.

PAROLLES
O Lord, sir, let me live, or let me see my death!

FIRST LORD

That shall you, and take your leave of all your friends.

Unblinding him

So, look about you: know you any here?

BERTRAM
Good morrow, noble captain.

SECOND LORD
God bless you, Captain Parolles.

FIRST LORD
God save you, noble captain.

SECOND LORD
Captain, what greeting will you to my Lord Lafeu?
I am for France.

FIRST LORD
Good captain, will you give me a copy of the sonnet you writ to Diana in behalf of the Count Rousillon? an I were not a very coward, I'd compel it of you: but fare you well.

Exeunt BERTRAM and LORDS

FIRST SOLDIER
You are undone, captain, all but your scarf; that has a knot on't yet

PAROLLES
Who cannot be crushed with a plot?

FIRST SOLDIER
If you could find out a country where but women were that had received so much shame, you might begin an impudent nation. Fare ye well, sir; I am for France too: we shall speak of you there.

Exit with SOLDIERS

PAROLLES
Yet am I thankful: if my heart were great,
'Twould burst at this. Captain I'll be no more;
But I will eat and drink, and sleep as soft
As captain shall: simply the thing I am
Shall make me live. Who knows himself a braggart,
Let him fear this, for it will come to pass
that every braggart shall be found an ass.
Rust, sword? cool, blushes! and, Parolles, live
Safest in shame! being fool'd, by foolery thrive!
There's place and means for every man alive.
I'll after them.

Exit

SCENE IV. Florence. The Widow's House.

Enter HELENA, Widow, and DIANA

HELENA
That you may well perceive I have not wrong'd you,
One of the greatest in the Christian world
Shall be my surety; 'fore whose throne 'tis needful,
Ere I can perfect mine intents, to kneel:
Time was, I did him a desired office,
Dear almost as his life; which gratitude
Through flinty Tartar's bosom would peep forth,
And answer, thanks: I duly am inform'd
His grace is at Marseilles; to which place
We have convenient convoy. You must know
I am supposed dead: the army breaking,
My husband hies him home; where, heaven aiding,
And by the leave of my good lord the king,
We'll be before our welcome.

Widow
Gentle madam,
You never had a servant to whose trust
Your business was more welcome.

HELENA
Nor you, mistress,
Ever a friend whose thoughts more truly labour
To recompense your love: doubt not but heaven
Hath brought me up to be your daughter's dower,
As it hath fated her to be my motive
And helper to a husband. But, O strange men!
That can such sweet use make of what they hate,
When saucy trusting of the cozen'd thoughts
Defiles the pitchy night: so lust doth play
With what it loathes for that which is away.
But more of this hereafter. You, Diana,
Under my poor instructions yet must suffer
Something in my behalf.

DIANA
Let death and honesty
Go with your impositions, I am yours
Upon your will to suffer.

HELENA
Yet, I pray you:
But with the word the time will bring on summer,

When briers shall have leaves as well as thorns,
And be as sweet as sharp. We must away;
Our wagon is prepared, and time revives us:
All's well that ends well; still the fine's the crown;
Whate'er the course, the end is the renown.

Exeunt

SCENE V. Rousillon. The Count's Palace.

Enter COUNTESS, LAFEU, and Clown

LAFEU
No, no, no, your son was misled with a snipt-taffeta fellow there, whose villanous saffron would have made all the unbaked and doughy youth of a nation in his colour: your daughter-in-law had been alive at this hour, and your son here at home, more advanced by the king than by that red-tailed humble-bee I speak of.

COUNTESS
I would I had not known him; it was the death of the most virtuous gentlewoman that ever nature had praise for creating. If she had partaken of my flesh, and cost me the dearest groans of a mother, I could not have owed her a more rooted love.

LAFEU
'Twas a good lady, 'twas a good lady: we may pick a thousand salads ere we light on such another herb.

CLOWN
Indeed, sir, she was the sweet marjoram of the salad, or rather, the herb of grace.

LAFEU
They are not herbs, you knave; they are nose-herbs.

CLOWN
I am no great Nebuchadnezzar, sir; I have not much skill in grass.

LAFEU
Whether dost thou profess thyself, a knave or a fool?

CLOWN
A fool, sir, at a woman's service, and a knave at a man's.

LAFEU
Your distinction?

CLOWN
I would cozen the man of his wife and do his service.

LAFEU

So you were a knave at his service, indeed.

CLOWN
And I would give his wife my bauble, sir, to do her service.

LAFEU
I will subscribe for thee, thou art both knave and fool.

CLOWN
At your service.

LAFEU
No, no, no.

CLOWN
Why, sir, if I cannot serve you, I can serve as great a prince as you are.

LAFEU
Who's that? a Frenchman?

CLOWN
Faith, sir, a' has an English name; but his fisnomy is more hotter in France than there.

LAFEU
What prince is that?

CLOWN
The black prince, sir; alias, the prince of darkness; alias, the devil.

LAFEU
Hold thee, there's my purse: I give thee not this to suggest thee from thy master thou talkest of; serve him still.

CLOWN
I am a woodland fellow, sir, that always loved a great fire; and the master I speak of ever keeps a good fire. But, sure, he is the prince of the world; let his nobility remain in's court. I am for the house with the narrow gate, which I take to be too little for pomp to enter: some that humble themselves may; but the many will be too chill and tender, and they'll be for the flowery way that leads to the broad gate and the great fire.

LAFEU
Go thy ways, I begin to be aweary of thee; and I tell thee so before, because I would not fall out with thee. Go thy ways: let my horses be well looked to, without any tricks.

CLOWN
If I put any tricks upon 'em, sir, they shall be
jades' tricks; which are their own right by the law of nature.

Exit

LAFEU

A shrewd knave and an unhappy.

COUNTESS
So he is. My lord that's gone made himself much sport out of him: by his authority he remains here, which he thinks is a patent for his sauciness; and, indeed, he has no pace, but runs where he will.

LAFEU
I like him well; 'tis not amiss. And I was about to tell you, since I heard of the good lady's death and that my lord your son was upon his return home, I moved the king my master to speak in the behalf of my daughter; which, in the minority of them both, his majesty, out of a self-gracious remembrance, did first propose: his highness hath promised me to do it: and, to stop up the displeasure he hath conceived against your son, there is no fitter matter. How does your ladyship like it?

COUNTESS
With very much content, my lord; and I wish it happily effected.

LAFEU
His highness comes post from Marseilles, of as able body as when he numbered thirty: he will be here to-morrow, or I am deceived by him that in such intelligence hath seldom failed.

COUNTESS
It rejoices me, that I hope I shall see him ere I die. I have letters that my son will be here to-night: I shall beseech your lordship to remain with me till they meet together.

LAFEU
Madam, I was thinking with what manners I might safely be admitted.

COUNTESS
You need but plead your honourable privilege.

LAFEU
Lady, of that I have made a bold charter; but I thank my God it holds yet.

Re-enter CLOWN

CLOWN
O madam, yonder's my lord your son with a patch of velvet on's face: whether there be a scar under't or no, the velvet knows; but 'tis a goodly patch of velvet: his left cheek is a cheek of two pile and a half, but his right cheek is worn bare.

LAFEU
A scar nobly got, or a noble scar, is a good livery of honour; so belike is that.

CLOWN
But it is your carbonadoed face.

LAFEU
Let us go see your son, I pray you: I long to talk with the young noble soldier.

CLOWN

Faith there's a dozen of 'em, with delicate fine hats and most courteous feathers, which bow the head and nod at every man.

Exeunt

ACT V

SCENE I. Marseilles. A Street.

Enter HELENA, Widow, and DIANA, with two Attendants

HELENA
But this exceeding posting day and night
Must wear your spirits low; we cannot help it:
But since you have made the days and nights as one,
To wear your gentle limbs in my affairs,
Be bold you do so grow in my requital
As nothing can unroot you. In happy time;

Enter a GENTLEMAN

This man may help me to his majesty's ear,
If he would spend his power. God save you, sir.

GENTLEMAN
And you.

HELENA
Sir, I have seen you in the court of France.

GENTLEMAN
I have been sometimes there.

HELENA
I do presume, sir, that you are not fallen
From the report that goes upon your goodness;
An therefore, goaded with most sharp occasions,
Which lay nice manners by, I put you to
The use of your own virtues, for the which
I shall continue thankful.

GENTLEMAN
What's your will?

HELENA
That it will please you
To give this poor petition to the king,
And aid me with that store of power you have
To come into his presence.

GENTLEMAN
The king's not here.

HELENA
Not here, sir!

GENTLEMAN
Not, indeed:
He hence removed last night and with more haste
Than is his use.

WIDOW
Lord, how we lose our pains!

HELENA
ALL'S WELL THAT ENDS WELL yet,
Though time seem so adverse and means unfit.
I do beseech you, whither is he gone?

GENTLEMAN
Marry, as I take it, to Rousillon;
Whither I am going.

HELENA
I do beseech you, sir,
Since you are like to see the king before me,
Commend the paper to his gracious hand,
Which I presume shall render you no blame
But rather make you thank your pains for it.
I will come after you with what good speed
Our means will make us means.

GENTLEMAN
This I'll do for you.

HELENA
And you shall find yourself to be well thank'd,
Whate'er falls more. We must to horse again.
Go, go, provide.

Exeunt

SCENE II. Rousillon. Before the Count's Palace.

Enter CLOWN, and PAROLLES, following

PAROLLES

Good Monsieur Lavache, give my Lord Lafeu this letter: I have ere now, sir, been better known to you, when I have held familiarity with fresher clothes; but I am now, sir, muddied in fortune's mood, and smell somewhat strong of her strong displeasure.

CLOWN
Truly, fortune's displeasure is but sluttish, if it smell so strongly as thou speakest of: I will henceforth eat no fish of fortune's buttering. Prithee, allow the wind.

PAROLLES
Nay, you need not to stop your nose, sir; I spake but by a metaphor.

CLOWN
Indeed, sir, if your metaphor stink, I will stop my nose; or against any man's metaphor. Prithee, get thee further.

PAROLLES
Pray you, sir, deliver me this paper.

CLOWN
Foh! prithee, stand away: a paper from fortune's close-stool to give to a nobleman! Look, here he comes himself.

Enter LAFEU

Here is a purr of fortune's, sir, or of fortune's cat,—but not a musk-cat,—that has fallen into the unclean fishpond of her displeasure, and, as he says, is muddied withal: pray you, sir, use the carp as you may; for he looks like a poor, decayed, ingenious, foolish, rascally knave. I do pity his distress in my similes of comfort and leave him to your lordship.

Exit

PAROLLES
My lord, I am a man whom fortune hath cruelly scratched.

LAFEU
And what would you have me to do? 'Tis too late to pare her nails now. Wherein have you played the knave with fortune, that she should scratch you, who of herself is a good lady and would not have knaves thrive long under her? There's a quart d'ecu for you: let the justices make you and fortune friends: I am for other business.

PAROLLES
I beseech your honour to hear me one single word.

LAFEU
You beg a single penny more: come, you shall ha't; save your word.

PAROLLES
My name, my good lord, is Parolles.

LAFEU
You beg more than 'word,' then. Cox my passion! give me your hand. How does your drum?

PAROLLES
O my good lord, you were the first that found me!

LAFEU
Was I, in sooth? and I was the first that lost thee.

PAROLLES
It lies in you, my lord, to bring me in some grace, for you did bring me out.

LAFEU
Out upon thee, knave! dost thou put upon me at once both the office of God and the devil? One brings thee in grace and the other brings thee out.

Trumpets sound

The king's coming; I know by his trumpets. Sirrah, inquire further after me; I had talk of you last night: though you are a fool and a knave, you shall eat; go to, follow.

PAROLLES
I praise God for you.

Exeunt

SCENE III. Rousillon. The Count's Palace.

Flourish. Enter KING, COUNTESS, LAFEU, the two French LORDS, with Attendants

KING
We lost a jewel of her; and our esteem
Was made much poorer by it: but your son,
As mad in folly, lack'd the sense to know
Her estimation home.

COUNTESS
'Tis past, my liege;
And I beseech your majesty to make it
Natural rebellion, done i' the blaze of youth;
When oil and fire, too strong for reason's force,
O'erbears it and burns on.

KING
My honour'd lady,
I have forgiven and forgotten all;
Though my revenges were high bent upon him,
And watch'd the time to shoot.

LAFEU

This I must say,
But first I beg my pardon, the young lord
Did to his majesty, his mother and his lady
Offence of mighty note; but to himself
The greatest wrong of all. He lost a wife
Whose beauty did astonish the survey
Of richest eyes, whose words all ears took captive,
Whose dear perfection hearts that scorn'd to serve
Humbly call'd mistress.

KING
Praising what is lost
Makes the remembrance dear. Well, call him hither;
We are reconciled, and the first view shall kill
All repetition: let him not ask our pardon;
The nature of his great offence is dead,
And deeper than oblivion we do bury
The incensing relics of it: let him approach,
A stranger, no offender; and inform him
So 'tis our will he should.

GENTLEMAN
I shall, my liege.

Exit

KING
What says he to your daughter? have you spoke?

LAFEU
All that he is hath reference to your highness.

KING
Then shall we have a match. I have letters sent me
That set him high in fame.

Enter BERTRAM

LAFEU
He looks well on't.

KING
I am not a day of season,
For thou mayst see a sunshine and a hail
In me at once: but to the brightest beams
Distracted clouds give way; so stand thou forth;
The time is fair again.

BERTRAM
My high-repented blames,
Dear sovereign, pardon to me.

KING
All is whole;
Not one word more of the consumed time.
Let's take the instant by the forward top;
For we are old, and on our quick'st decrees
The inaudible and noiseless foot of Time
Steals ere we can effect them. You remember
The daughter of this lord?

BERTRAM
Admiringly, my liege, at first
I stuck my choice upon her, ere my heart
Durst make too bold a herald of my tongue
Where the impression of mine eye infixing,
Contempt his scornful perspective did lend me,
Which warp'd the line of every other favour;
Scorn'd a fair colour, or express'd it stolen;
Extended or contracted all proportions
To a most hideous object: thence it came
That she whom all men praised and whom myself,
Since I have lost, have loved, was in mine eye
The dust that did offend it.

KING
Well excused:
That thou didst love her, strikes some scores away
From the great compt: but love that comes too late,
Like a remorseful pardon slowly carried,
To the great sender turns a sour offence,
Crying, 'That's good that's gone.' Our rash faults
Make trivial price of serious things we have,
Not knowing them until we know their grave:
Oft our displeasures, to ourselves unjust,
Destroy our friends and after weep their dust
Our own love waking cries to see what's done,
While shame full late sleeps out the afternoon.
Be this sweet Helen's knell, and now forget her.
Send forth your amorous token for fair Maudlin:
The main consents are had; and here we'll stay
To see our widower's second marriage-day.

COUNTESS
Which better than the first, O dear heaven, bless!
Or, ere they meet, in me, O nature, cesse!

LAFEU
Come on, my son, in whom my house's name
Must be digested, give a favour from you
To sparkle in the spirits of my daughter,
That she may quickly come.

BERTRAM gives a ring

By my old beard,
And every hair that's on't, Helen, that's dead,
Was a sweet creature: such a ring as this,
The last that e'er I took her at court,
I saw upon her finger.

BERTRAM
Hers it was not.

KING
Now, pray you, let me see it; for mine eye,
While I was speaking, oft was fasten'd to't.
This ring was mine; and, when I gave it Helen,
I bade her, if her fortunes ever stood
Necessitied to help, that by this token
I would relieve her. Had you that craft, to reave her
Of what should stead her most?

BERTRAM
My gracious sovereign,
Howe'er it pleases you to take it so,
The ring was never hers.

COUNTESS
Son, on my life,
I have seen her wear it; and she reckon'd it
At her life's rate.

LAFEU
I am sure I saw her wear it.

BERTRAM
You are deceived, my lord; she never saw it:
In Florence was it from a casement thrown me,
Wrapp'd in a paper, which contain'd the name
Of her that threw it: noble she was, and thought
I stood engaged: but when I had subscribed
To mine own fortune and inform'd her fully
I could not answer in that course of honour
As she had made the overture, she ceased
In heavy satisfaction and would never
Receive the ring again.

KING
Plutus himself,
That knows the tinct and multiplying medicine,
Hath not in nature's mystery more science
Than I have in this ring: 'twas mine, 'twas Helen's,

Whoever gave it you. Then, if you know
That you are well acquainted with yourself,
Confess 'twas hers, and by what rough enforcement
You got it from her: she call'd the saints to surety
That she would never put it from her finger,
Unless she gave it to yourself in bed,
Where you have never come, or sent it us
Upon her great disaster.

BERTRAM
She never saw it.

KING
Thou speak'st it falsely, as I love mine honour;
And makest conjectural fears to come into me
Which I would fain shut out. If it should prove
That thou art so inhuman,—'twill not prove so;—
And yet I know not: thou didst hate her deadly,
And she is dead; which nothing, but to close
Her eyes myself, could win me to believe,
More than to see this ring. Take him away.

Guards seize BERTRAM

My fore-past proofs, howe'er the matter fall,
Shall tax my fears of little vanity,
Having vainly fear'd too little. Away with him!
We'll sift this matter further.

BERTRAM
If you shall prove
This ring was ever hers, you shall as easy
Prove that I husbanded her bed in Florence,
Where yet she never was.

Exit, guarded

KING
I am wrapp'd in dismal thinkings.

Enter a GENTLEMAN

GENTLEMAN
Gracious sovereign,
Whether I have been to blame or no, I know not:
Here's a petition from a Florentine,
Who hath for four or five removes come short
To tender it herself. I undertook it,
Vanquish'd thereto by the fair grace and speech
Of the poor suppliant, who by this I know
Is here attending: her business looks in her

With an importing visage; and she told me,
In a sweet verbal brief, it did concern
Your highness with herself.

KING
[Reads] Upon his many protestations to marry me when his wife was dead, I blush to say it, he won me. Now is the Count Rousillon a widower: his vows are forfeited to me, and my honour's paid to him. He stole from Florence, taking no leave, and I follow him to his country for justice: grant it me, O king! in you it best lies; otherwise a seducer flourishes, and a poor maid is undone.
DIANA CAPILET.

LAFEU
I will buy me a son-in-law in a fair, and toll for this: I'll none of him.

KING
The heavens have thought well on thee Lafeu,
To bring forth this discovery. Seek these suitors:
Go speedily and bring again the count.
I am afeard the life of Helen, lady,
Was foully snatch'd.

COUNTESS
Now, justice on the doers!

Re-enter BERTRAM, guarded

KING
I wonder, sir, sith wives are monsters to you,
And that you fly them as you swear them lordship,
Yet you desire to marry.

Enter Widow and DIANA

What woman's that?

DIANA
I am, my lord, a wretched Florentine,
Derived from the ancient Capilet:
My suit, as I do understand, you know,
And therefore know how far I may be pitied.

WIDOW
I am her mother, sir, whose age and honour
Both suffer under this complaint we bring,
And both shall cease, without your remedy.

KING
Come hither, count; do you know these women?

BERTRAM

My lord, I neither can nor will deny
But that I know them: do they charge me further?

DIANA
Why do you look so strange upon your wife?

BERTRAM
She's none of mine, my lord.

DIANA
If you shall marry,
You give away this hand, and that is mine;
You give away heaven's vows, and those are mine;
You give away myself, which is known mine;
For I by vow am so embodied yours,
That she which marries you must marry me,
Either both or none.

LAFEU
Your reputation comes too short for my daughter; you are no husband for her.

BERTRAM
My lord, this is a fond and desperate creature,
Whom sometime I have laugh'd with: let your highness
Lay a more noble thought upon mine honour
Than for to think that I would sink it here.

KING
Sir, for my thoughts, you have them ill to friend
Till your deeds gain them: fairer prove your honour
Than in my thought it lies.

DIANA
Good my lord,
Ask him upon his oath, if he does think
He had not my virginity.

KING
What say'st thou to her?

BERTRAM
She's impudent, my lord,
And was a common gamester to the camp.

DIANA
He does me wrong, my lord; if I were so,
He might have bought me at a common price:
Do not believe him. O, behold this ring,
Whose high respect and rich validity
Did lack a parallel; yet for all that

He gave it to a commoner o' the camp,
If I be one.

COUNTESS
He blushes, and 'tis it:
Of six preceding ancestors, that gem,
Conferr'd by testament to the sequent issue,
Hath it been owed and worn. This is his wife;
That ring's a thousand proofs.

KING
Methought you said
You saw one here in court could witness it.

DIANA
I did, my lord, but loath am to produce
So bad an instrument: his name's Parolles.

LAFEU
I saw the man to-day, if man he be.

KING
Find him, and bring him hither.

Exit an ATTENDANT

BERTRAM
What of him?
He's quoted for a most perfidious slave,
With all the spots o' the world tax'd and debosh'd;
Whose nature sickens but to speak a truth.
Am I or that or this for what he'll utter,
That will speak any thing?

KING
She hath that ring of yours.

BERTRAM
I think she has: certain it is I liked her,
And boarded her i' the wanton way of youth:
She knew her distance and did angle for me,
Madding my eagerness with her restraint,
As all impediments in fancy's course
Are motives of more fancy; and, in fine,
Her infinite cunning, with her modern grace,
Subdued me to her rate: she got the ring;
And I had that which any inferior might
At market-price have bought.

DIANA

I must be patient:
You, that have turn'd off a first so noble wife,
May justly diet me. I pray you yet;
Since you lack virtue, I will lose a husband;
Send for your ring, I will return it home,
And give me mine again.

BERTRAM
I have it not.

KING
What ring was yours, I pray you?

DIANA
Sir, much like
The same upon your finger.

KING
Know you this ring? this ring was his of late.

DIANA
And this was it I gave him, being abed.

KING
The story then goes false, you threw it him
Out of a casement.

DIANA
I have spoke the truth.

Enter PAROLLES

BERTRAM
My lord, I do confess the ring was hers.

KING
You boggle shrewdly, every feather stars you.
Is this the man you speak of?

DIANA
Ay, my lord.

KING
Tell me, sirrah, but tell me true, I charge you,
Not fearing the displeasure of your master,
Which on your just proceeding I'll keep off,
By him and by this woman here what know you?

PAROLLES
So please your majesty, my master hath been an honourable gentleman: tricks he hath had in him, which gentlemen have.

KING
Come, come, to the purpose: did he love this woman?

PAROLLES
Faith, sir, he did love her; but how?

KING
How, I pray you?

PAROLLES
He did love her, sir, as a gentleman loves a woman.

KING
How is that?

PAROLLES
He loved her, sir, and loved her not.

KING
As thou art a knave, and no knave. What an equivocal companion is this!

PAROLLES
I am a poor man, and at your majesty's command.

LAFEU
He's a good drum, my lord, but a naughty orator.

DIANA
Do you know he promised me marriage?

PAROLLES
Faith, I know more than I'll speak.

KING
But wilt thou not speak all thou knowest?

PAROLLES
Yes, so please your majesty. I did go between them, as I said; but more than that, he loved her: for indeed he was mad for her, and talked of Satan and of Limbo and of Furies and I know not what: yet I was in that credit with them at that time that I knew of their going to bed, and of other motions, as promising her marriage, and things which would derive me ill will to speak of; therefore I will not speak what I know.

KING
Thou hast spoken all already, unless thou canst say they are married: but thou art too fine in thy evidence; therefore stand aside. This ring, you say, was yours?

DIANA
Ay, my good lord.

KING
Where did you buy it? or who gave it you?

DIANA
It was not given me, nor I did not buy it.

KING
Who lent it you?

DIANA
It was not lent me neither.

KING
Where did you find it, then?

DIANA
I found it not.

KING
If it were yours by none of all these ways,
How could you give it him?

DIANA
I never gave it him.

LAFEU
This woman's an easy glove, my lord; she goes off and on at pleasure.

KING
This ring was mine; I gave it his first wife.

DIANA
It might be yours or hers, for aught I know.

KING
Take her away; I do not like her now;
To prison with her: and away with him.
Unless thou tell'st me where thou hadst this ring,
Thou diest within this hour.

DIANA
I'll never tell you.

KING
Take her away.

DIANA
I'll put in bail, my liege.

KING
I think thee now some common customer.

DIANA
By Jove, if ever I knew man, 'twas you.

KING
Wherefore hast thou accused him all this while?

DIANA
Because he's guilty, and he is not guilty:
He knows I am no maid, and he'll swear to't;
I'll swear I am a maid, and he knows not.
Great king, I am no strumpet, by my life;
I am either maid, or else this old man's wife.

KING
She does abuse our ears: to prison with her.

DIANA
Good mother, fetch my bail. Stay, royal sir:

Exit WIDOW

The jeweller that owes the ring is sent for,
And he shall surety me. But for this lord,
Who hath abused me, as he knows himself,
Though yet he never harm'd me, here I quit him:
He knows himself my bed he hath defiled;
And at that time he got his wife with child:
Dead though she be, she feels her young one kick:
So there's my riddle: one that's dead is quick:
And now behold the meaning.

Re-enter WIDOW, with HELENA

KING
Is there no exorcist
Beguiles the truer office of mine eyes?
Is't real that I see?

HELENA
No, my good lord;
'Tis but the shadow of a wife you see,
The name and not the thing.

BERTRAM
Both, both. O, pardon!

HELENA
O my good lord, when I was like this maid,
I found you wondrous kind. There is your ring;
And, look you, here's your letter; this it says:

'When from my finger you can get this ring
And are by me with child,' & c. This is done:
Will you be mine, now you are doubly won?

BERTRAM
If she, my liege, can make me know this clearly,
I'll love her dearly, ever, ever dearly.

HELENA
If it appear not plain and prove untrue,
Deadly divorce step between me and you!
O my dear mother, do I see you living?

LAFEU
Mine eyes smell onions; I shall weep anon:

To PAROLLES

Good Tom Drum, lend me a handkercher: so,
I thank thee: wait on me home, I'll make sport with thee:
Let thy courtesies alone, they are scurvy ones.

KING
Let us from point to point this story know,
To make the even truth in pleasure flow.

To DIANA

If thou be'st yet a fresh uncropped flower,
Choose thou thy husband, and I'll pay thy dower;
For I can guess that by thy honest aid
Thou keep'st a wife herself, thyself a maid.
Of that and all the progress, more or less,
Resolvedly more leisure shall express:
All yet seems well; and if it end so meet,
The bitter past, more welcome is the sweet.

Flourish

KING
The king's a beggar, now the play is done:
All is well ended, if this suit be won,
That you express content; which we will pay,
With strife to please you, day exceeding day:
Ours be your patience then, and yours our parts;
Your gentle hands lend us, and take our hearts.

Exeunt

William Shakespeare – A Short Biography

The life of William Shakespeare, arguably the most significant figure in the Western literary canon, is relatively unknown. Even the exact date of his birth is uncertain. April 23rd, the date now generally accepted to be the date of his birth, is a result of a scholarly mistake and the appealing coincidence of its being also the day of his death.

That so little is known about a writer with such great literary scope and accomplishment has naturally invited speculation and conspiracy theories about the authenticity of his authorship, his influence and even his existence.

Shakespeare was born in Stratford-upon-Avon in 1565, possibly on the 23rd April, St. George's Day, and baptised there on 26th April. His father was John Shakespeare, a successful glover and alderman who hailed from Snitterfield. His mother was Mary Arden, whose father was an affluent landowner. In total their union bore eight children; William was the third of these and the eldest surviving son.

Although there is no hard evidence on his education it is widely agreed among scholars that William attended the King's New School in Stratford which was chartered as a free school in 1553. This school was only a quarter of a mile from the house in which he spent his childhood, but since there are no attendance records existing it is assumed, rather than known, this was the base for his education.

Although the quality of education in a grammar school at that time varied wildly the curriculum did not, a key aspect of which, by royal decree, was Latin, and it is undoubtable that the school will have delivered an intensive education in Latin grammar, drawing heavily on the work of the classical Latin authors. If Shakespeare did attend this school then it is very likely the starting point for the fascination with and extensive knowledge of the classical Latin authors which would inform and inspire so much of his work began.

Little more detail is known of William's childhood, or his early teenage years, until, at the age of 18, he married Anne Hathaway, who was 26 and from the nearby village of Shottery. Her father was a yeoman farmer, and their family home a small farmhouse in the village. In his will he left her £6 13s 4d, six pounds, thirteen shillings and fourpence, to be paid on her wedding day. On November 27th, 1582 the consistory court of the Diocese of Worcester issued a marriage licence, and on the 28th two of Hathaway's neighbours, Fulk Sandells and John Richardson, posted bonds which guaranteed that there were no lawful claims to impede the marriage along with a surety of £40 to act as a financial guarantee for the wedding.

The marriage was conducted in some haste since, unusually, the marriage banns were read only once instead of the more normal three times, a decision which would have been taken by the Worcester chancellor. This haste is no doubt due to the child Anne delivered their first child, Susanna, six months later. Susanna, was baptised on May 26th, 1583. Several scholars have voiced their opinion that the wedding was imposed on a reluctant Shakespeare by Hathaway's outraged parents, although, again, there is nothing to formally support the theory. It has been further argued that the circumstances surrounding the wedding, particularly those of the neighbourly assurances, indicate that Shakespeare was involved with two women at the time of his marriage. According to the theory proposed by the early twentieth century scholar Frank Harris, Shakespeare had already chosen to marry a woman named Anne Whateley. It was only once this proposed union became known that Hathaway's outraged family forced him to marry their daughter. Harris goes on to surmise that Shakespeare considered the affair entrapment, and that this led to his wholesale despising of her, a "loathing for his wife [which] was measureless" and which ultimately caused him to leave Stratford and her and make for the theatre. But equally other scholars such as John Aubrey have responded to this with evidence that Shakespeare returned to Stratford every year which, if true, would rather diminish Harris's claim that Hathaway had poisoned Stratford for Shakespeare.

Harris's theory aside, Shakespeare and Hathaway had two more children, twins Hamnet and Judith, baptised on February 2nd,1585. Hamnet, Shakespeare's only son, died during one of the frequent outbreaks of bubonic plague and was buried on the August 11th, 1596, at the age of only eleven.

Little is known of Shakespeare's life during the years following the birth of the twins until he appears mentioned in relation to the London theatres in 1592, apart from a fleeting mention in the complaints bill of a legal case which came before the Queen's Bench court at Westminster, dated Michaelmas Term 1588 and October 9th, 1589. Despite this period of time being referred to in scholarly circles as Shakespeare's "lost years", there are several stories, apocryphal in nature, which are attributed to Shakespeare. For example, there is a legend in Stratford that he fled the town in order to avoid prosecution for poaching deer on the estate of Thomas Lucy, a local squire. It is also supposed that Shakespeare went so far as to take revenge on Lucy, a politician whose Protestantism opposed Shakespeare's Catholic childhood, by writing the following lampooning ballad about him:

> A parliament member, a justice of peace,
> At home a poor scarecrow, at London an ass,
> If lousy is Lucy as some folks miscall it
> Then Lucy is lousy whatever befall it.

However amusing the ballad and legend may be in imagining the life of a young Shakespeare, youthfully mischievous and still developing the wit, sense of adventure and humour which would become integral aspects of his writing, there is simply no evidence either to support the theory or to suggest that Shakespeare penned the ballad. Alongside this are suggestions that he began his theatrical career while minding the horses of the patrons of the London theatres and that he spent some time as a schoolmaster employed by one Alexander Hoghton, a Catholic landowner in Lancashire, in whose will is named "William Shakeshafte". However, this was a popular name in the Lancashire area at that time and there is no evidence that this referred to Shakespeare. The wealth of his writing makes it a frustrating exercise to learn more of his life and the manner in which he achieved those outstanding and lionized works.

Interestingly, the reference to Shakespeare in 1592 which ends the "lost years" is a piece of theatrical criticism by playwright Robert Greene in *Groats-Worth of Wit*. In a scathing passage Greene writes "...there is an upstart Crow, beautified with our feathers, that with his *Tiger's heart wrapped in a Player's hide*, supposes he is as well able to bombast out a blank verse as the best of you: and being an absolute *Johannes factotum*, is in his own conceit the only Shake-scene in a country." From this entry we can make some important inferences which shed light on Shakespeare's career, the first of which is that to be acknowledged, even negatively, by a playwright such as Robert Greene, by this point he must have been making significant impact on the London stage as a writer. Also of significance is the very meaning of the words themselves, for it is generally acknowledged that Shakespeare is being accused of writing with a lofty ambition beyond his capabilities and, more importantly, the capabilities of his contemporaries who were educated at Oxford and Cambridge. Within this remark, then, is an inherent snobbery which Shakespeare would come to resent and ultimately challenge in his writing. Though Greene's parody of "Oh, tiger's heart wrapped in a woman's hide" makes reference to *Henry VI, Part 3*, it is likely that Greene's opinion of Shakespeare was in part informed by another of Shakespeare's plays which was heavily criticised, *Titus Adronicus*, believed to have been written between 1588 and 1593. It was his first attempt at tragedy, almost prototypical, and was written at a time when, according to the scholar Jonathan Bate, he was "experimenting with ways of writing about and representing rape and seduction". Drawing heavily on the sixth book of Ovid's *Metamorphoses* as its main source of inspiration for the rape and mutilation of Lavinia, it offended the sensibilities of the more highbrow members of its audience, whilst presumably also simultaneously intimidating them with its detailed knowledge of Ovid, a writer typically considered the reserve of the university-educated. Not only, then, was Shakespeare demonstrating a knowledge of classical literature which they thought befitted only a traditional scholar and thereby shining a light to the snobbery and exclusivity of such an education, but he was doing it radically and brilliantly.

By 1594 the Lord Chamberlain's Men had recognised his worthiness as a playwright and were performing his works. With the advantage of Shakespeare's progressive writing they rapidly became London's leading company of players, affording him more exposure and, following the death of Queen Elizabeth in 1603, a royal patent by the new king, James I, at which point they changed their name to the King's Men.

Before this success, though, several company members had formed a partnership to build their own theatre which came to be on the south bank of the river Thames, the now-famous and reconstructed Globe theatre. Though it is unclear precisely what Shakespeare's involvement in this venture was, records of his property and investments indicate that he came to be rich during this period, buying the second-largest house in Stratford, called New Place, in 1597, which he made his family home. Prior to this he was living in the parish of St Helen's Bishopsgate, north of the River Thames. He continued to spend most of his time at work in London and from about 1598-1602, he seems to have lived in the Paris Gardens area of Bankside south of the river near The Globe.

Despite efforts to pirate his work, Shakespeare's name was by 1598 so well known that it had already become a selling point in its own right on title pages.

An interesting aside is that theatres were mostly constructed on the south bank of the Thames (then part of the county of Surrey) as performing in London itself was thought to be a bad influence on the masses and subject to periodic bouts of censorship, repression and closing of venues which in the City itself was mainly courtyards and open areas at the many Inns.

Excluded from the City purpose built theatres began to be constructed outside the City limits. This area of the Thames though was rough and naturally vibrant with all sorts of characters, many of them of dubious nature or even criminal. It was also prone, due to its over-crowding and bad sanitation, to bouts of bubonic plague and other diseases particularly during the summer which was a further reason for the theatres there being closed. The Curtain, The Rose, The Swan, The Fortune, The Blackfriars and of course The Globe were all purpose built and situated here, some with an audience capacity approaching 3,000.

The first known printed copies of Shakespeare's plays date from 1594 in quarto editions, though these quarto editions are often considered "bad", a term referring to the likelihood of specific quarto editions being based on, for example, a reconstruction of a play as it was witnessed, rather than Shakespeare's original manuscript. The best example of such memorial reconstruction can be found in the differences between the first and second quarto editions of *Hamlet*. In examining Hamlet's most famous soliloquy, "to be or not to be", we can immediately recognise significant differences. First, the familiar second quarto version:

> To be, or not to be; that is the question:
> Whether 'tis nobler in the mind to suffer

> The slings and arrows of outrageous fortune,
> Or to take arms against a sea of troubles,
> And, by opposing, end them.

And, by contrast, the first quarto version:

> To be, or not to be, I there's the point,
> To Die, to sleep, is that all? I all:

For scholar Henry David Gray the first quarto lines are emblematic of "a distorted version of the completed drama filled out and revised by an inferior poet" and based, he goes on to argue, on the fractured memories of the play as witnessed and performed by the actor playing Marcellus. Gray, and several other critics, consider the first quarto a pirated copy, printed in haste without the writer's permission in an attempt to make quick money following the success of the play in the theatre. In understanding the significance of Marcellus to the theory it is imperative to note that the authenticity of each quarto is based on its similarities to the version of the play found in the first folio, printed in 1623 and believed to be authorised by Shakespeare. Therefore, since in the folio version of *Hamlet* the "to be or not to be" soliloquy is virtually identical to that of the second quarto, it is believed that the second was authored by Shakespeare himself and that the first, by its considerable differences, must therefore be in some way compromised. However, when read in comparison to the folio version, the only character whose lines are almost entirely perfect are those spoken by Marcellus, which, since dramatic practice at the time was for actors to be given only their own lines and three or four word 'cues' based on the lines preceding theirs, suggests that the first quarto is a memorial reconstruction of the play written by the actor who played Marcellus. Having committed his own lines to memory he was able to reproduce them accurately, but was left to fill in the remaining lines and plot from memory which accounts for the truncated and often vastly inferior writing in the first quarto.

According to the remaining cast lists from the period, Shakespeare remained an actor throughout his career as a writer, and it is thought he continued to act after he retired his pen. In 1616 he is recorded in the cast list in Ben Jonson's collected *Works* in the plays *Man in His Humour* 1598) and *Sejanus His Fall* (1603), though some scholars consider his absence from the list of Jonson's *Volpone* evidence that, by 1605, his acting career was nearing its end. Despite this in the First Folio he is listed as one of "the Principle Actors in all these Plays", several of which were only staged after *Volpone*.

By 1604 he had moved again, remaining north of the river, to an area near St. Paul's Cathedral where he rented a fine room amongst fine houses from Christopher Mountjoy, a French hatmaker and Huguenot.

The Anglo-Welsh poet John Davies of Hereford wrote in 1610 that "good Will" tended to play "kingly" roles, suggesting he was still on stage, perhaps now performing the more mature kings such as Lear and Henry VI. There has even been the suggestion that Shakespeare played the ghost of Hamlet's father, though there is little evidence to suggest it.

In 1608 the King's Men purchased the Blackfriars theatre from Henry Evans, and according to Cuthbert Burbage, one of the most highly regarded actors of the time, "placed many players" there "which were Hemminges, Condell, Shakespeare, etc." A 1609 lawsuit brought against John Addenbrooke in Stratford on the 7th of June describes Shakespeare as "generosus nuper in curia domini Jacobi" (a gentleman recently at the court of King James) which indicates that by this time he was spending more time in Stratford. A likely cause of this was the bubonic plague, frequent outbreaks of which demanded the equally frequent closing of places of public gathering, principle among which were the theatres. Between May 1603 and February 1610 the theatres were closed for a total of 60 months, meaning there was no acting work and nobody to perform new plays. Though in 1610 Shakespeare returned to Stratford and it is supposed lived with his wife, he made frequent visits to London between 1611-14, being called as a witness in the trial *Bellott v. Mountjoy*, a case addressing concerns about the marriage settlement of Mountjoy's daughter, Mary. In March 1613 he purchased a gatehouse in the former Blackfriars priory, and spent several weeks in the city with his son-in-law John Hall, a physician, married to his daughter Susanna, from November 1614.

No plays are attributed to Shakespeare after 1613, and the last few plays he wrote before this time were in collaboration with other writers, one of whom is likely to be John Fletcher who succeeded him as the house playwright for the King's Men.

In early 1616 his daughter Judith married Thomas Quiney, a vintner and tobacconist. He signed his last will and testament on March 25th, of the same year, and the following day Quiney was ordered to do public penance for having fathered an illegitimate child with a woman named Margaret Wheeler who had died during childbirth which had enabled Quiney to cover up the scandal. This public humiliation would have been embarrassing for Shakespeare and his family.

William Shakespeare died two months later on April 23rd, 1616, survived by his wife and two daughters.

According to his will the bulk of his considerable estate was left to his elder daughter Susanna, with the instruction that she pass it down intact to "the first son of her body". However, though Susanna and Judith had four children between them they all died without progeny, ending Shakespeare's direct lineage. Also in his will was the instruction that his "second best bed" be left to his wife Anne, likely an insult, though the bed was possibly matrimonial and therefore of significant sentimental value.

He was buried two days after his death in the chancel of the Holy Trinity Church in Stratford-Upon-Avon.

The epitaph on the slab which covers his grave includes the following passage,

> Good frend for Iesvs sake forbeare,
> To digg the dvst encloased heare.
> Bleste be ye man yt spares thes stones,
> And cvrst be he yt moves my bones

which, in modern translation, reads

> Good friend, for Jesus's sake forbear,
> To dig the dust enclosed here.
> Blessed be the man that spares these stones,
> And cursed be he that moves my bones.

At some point before 1623 there was a funerary monument erected in his memory on the north wall of Stratford-upon-Avon which features a half-effigy of him writing, and which likens him to Nestor, Socrates and Virgil.

On January 29th, 1741 a white marble memorial statue to him was erected in Poets' Corner in Westminster Abbey.

Though there have been many monuments built around the world in memory of Shakespeare, undoubtedly the greatest memorial of all is the body of work which became the foundation of Western literary canon and an inspiration for every generation.

William Shakespeare – A Concise Bibliography

1589	Comedy of Errors (Comedy)
1590	Henry VI, Part II (History)
	Henry VI, Part III (History)
1591	Henry VI, Part I (History)
1592	Richard III (History)
1593	Taming of the Shrew (Comedy)
	Titus Andronicus (Tragedy)
	Venus and Adonis (Poem)
1594	Rape of Lucrece (Poem)
	Romeo and Juliet (Tragedy)
	Two Gentlemen of Verona (Comedy)
	Love's Labour's Lost (Comedy)
1595	Richard II (History)
	Midsummer Night's Dream (Comedy)
1596	King John (History)
	Merchant of Venice (Comedy)
1597	Henry IV, Part I (History)
	Henry IV, Part II (History)
1598	Passionate Pilgrim (Poem)
	Henry V (History)
	Much Ado about Nothing (Comedy)
1599	Twelfth Night (Comedy)
	As You Like It (Comedy)
	Julius Caesar (Tragedy)
1600	Hamlet (Tragedy)
	Merry Wives of Windsor (Comedy)
1601	Troilus and Cressida (Comedy)
1601	Phoenix and the Turtle (Poem))

1602	All's Well That Ends Well (Comedy)
1604	Othello (Tragedy)
	Measure for Measure
1605	King Lear (Tragedy)
	Macbeth (Tragedy)
1606	Antony and Cleopatra (Tragedy)
1607	Coriolanus (Tragedy)
	Timon of Athens (Tragedy)
1608	Pericles (Comedy)
1609	Cymbeline (Comedy)
	Lover's Complaint (Poem)
1610	Winter's Tale (Comedy)
1611	Tempest (Comedy)
1612	Henry VIII (History)

As regards his 154 sonnets it is almost impossible to date each individually though collectively they were first published in 1609, with two having been published in 1599.

Shakspeare; or, the Poet by Ralph Waldo Emerson

Great (1) men are more distinguished by range and extent than by originality. If we require the originality which consists in weaving, like a spider, their web from their own bowels; in finding clay and making bricks and building the house; no great men are original. Nor does valuable originality consist in unlikeness to other men. The hero is in the press of knights and the thick of events; and seeing what men want and sharing their desire, he adds the needful length of sight and of arm, to come at the desired point. The greatest genius is the most indebted man. A poet is no rattle-brain, saying what comes uppermost, and, because he says every thing, saying at last something good; but a heart in unison with his time and country. There is nothing whimsical and fantastic in his production, but sweet and sad earnest, freighted with the weightiest convictions and pointed with the most determined aim which any man or class knows of in his times. (2)

The Genius of our life is jealous of individuals, and will not have any individual great, except through the general. There is no choice to genius. A great man does not wake up on some fine morning and say, 'I am full of life, I will go to sea and find an Antarctic continent: to-day I will square the circle: I will ransack botany and find a new food for man: I have a new architecture in my mind: I foresee a new mechanic power:' no, but he finds himself in the river of the thoughts and events, forced onward by the ideas and necessities of his contemporaries. (3) He stands where all the eyes of men look one way, and their hands all point in the direction in which he should go. The Church has reared him amidst rites and pomps, and he carries out the advice which her music gave him, and builds a cathedral needed by her chants and processions. He finds a war raging: it educates him, by trumpet, in barracks, and he betters the instruction. He finds two counties groping to bring coal, or flour, or fish, from the place of production to the place of consumption, and he hits on a railroad. Every master has found his materials collected, and his power lay in his sympathy with his people and in his love of the materials he wrought in. What an economy of power! and what a compensation for the shortness of life! All is done to his hand. The world has brought him thus far on his way. The human race has gone out before him, sunk the hills, filled the hollows and bridged the rivers. Men, nations, poets, artisans, women, all have worked for him, and he enters into their labors. Choose any other thing, out of the line of tendency, out of the national feeling and history, and he would have all to do for himself: his powers would be expended in the first preparations. Great genial power, one would almost say, consists in not being original at all; in being altogether receptive; in letting the world do all, and suffering the spirit of the hour to pass unobstructed through the mind. (4)

Shakspeare's youth fell in a time when the English people were importunate for dramatic entertainments. The court took offence easily at political allusions and attempted to suppress them. The Puritans, a growing and energetic party, and the religious among the Anglican church, would suppress them. But the people wanted them. Inn-yards, houses without roofs, and extemporaneous enclosures at country fairs were the ready theatres of strolling players. The people had tasted this new joy; and, as we could not hope to suppress newspapers now,—no, not by the strongest party,—neither then could king, prelate, or puritan, alone or united, suppress an organ which was ballad, epic, newspaper, caucus, lecture, Punch and library, at the same time. Probably king, prelate and puritan, all found their own account in it. It had become, by all causes, a national interest,—by no means conspicuous, so that some great scholar would have thought of treating it in an English history,—but not a whit less considerable because it was cheap and of no account, like a baker's-shop. The best proof of its vitality is the crowd of writers which suddenly broke into this field; Kyd, Marlow, Greene, Jonson, Chapman, Dekker, Webster, Heywood, Middleton, Peele, Ford, Massinger, Beaumont and Fletcher.

The secure possession, by the stage, of the public mind, is of the first importance to the poet who works for it. (5) He loses no time in idle experiments. Here is audience and expectation prepared. In the case of Shakspeare there is much more. At the time when he left Stratford and went up to London, a great body of stage-plays of all dates and writers existed in manuscript and were in turn produced on the boards. Here is the Tale of Troy, which the audience will bear hearing some part of, every week; the Death of Julius Cæsar, and other stories out of Plutarch, which they never tire of; a shelf full of English history, from the chronicles of Brut and Arthur, down to the royal Henries, which men hear eagerly; and a string of doleful tragedies, merry Italian tales and Spanish voyages, which all the London 'prentices know. All the mass has been treated, with more or less skill, by every playwright, and the prompter has the soiled and tattered manuscripts. It is now no longer possible to say who wrote them first. They have been the property of the Theatre so long, and so many rising geniuses have enlarged or altered them, inserting a speech or a whole scene, or adding a song, that no man can any longer claim copyright in this work of numbers. Happily, no man wishes to. They are not yet desired in that way. We have few readers, many spectators and hearers. They had best lie where they are.

Shakspeare, in common with his comrades, esteemed the mass of old plays waste stock, in which any experiment could be freely tried. Had the prestige which hedges about a modern tragedy existed, nothing could have been done. The rude warm blood of the living England circulated in the play, as in street-ballads, and gave body which he wanted to his airy and majestic fancy. The poet needs a ground in popular tradition on which he may work, and which, again, may restrain his art within the due temperance. It holds him to the people, supplies a foundation for his edifice, and in furnishing so much work done to his hand, leaves him at leisure and in full strength for the audacities of his imagination. In short, the poet owes to his legend what sculpture owed to the temple. Sculpture in Egypt and in Greece grew up in subordination to architecture. It was the ornament of the temple wall: at first a rude relief carved on pediments, then the relief became bolder and a head or arm was projected from the wall; the groups being still arranged with reference to the building, which serves also as a frame to hold the figures; and when at last the greatest freedom of style and treatment was reached, the prevailing genius of architecture still enforced a certain calmness and continence in the statue. As soon as the statue was begun for itself, and with no reference to the temple or palace, the art began to decline: freak, extravagance and exhibition took the place of the old temperance. This balance-wheel, which the sculptor found in architecture, the perilous irritability of poetic talent found in the accumulated dramatic materials to which the people were already wonted, and which had a certain excellence which no single genius, however extraordinary, could hope to create.

In point of fact it appears that Shakspeare did owe debts in all directions, and was able to use whatever he found; and the amount of indebtedness may be inferred from Malone's laborious computations in regard to the First, Second and Third parts of Henry VI., in which, "out of 6043 lines, 1771 were written by some author preceding Shakspeare, 2373 by him, on the foundation laid by his predecessors, and 1899 were entirely his own." And the proceeding investigation hardly leaves a single drama of his absolute invention. Malone's sentence is an important piece of external history. In Henry VIII. I think I see plainly the cropping out of the original rock on which his own finer stratum was laid. The first play was written by a superior, thoughtful man, with a vicious ear. I can mark his lines, and know well their cadence. See Wolsey's soliloquy, and the following scene with Cromwell, where instead of the metre of Shakspeare, whose secret is that the thought constructs the tune, so that reading for the sense will best bring out the rhythm,—here the lines are constructed on a given tune, and the verse has even a trace of pulpit eloquence. But the play contains through all its length unmistakable traits of Shakspeare's hand, and some passages, as the account of the coronation, are like autographs. What is odd, the compliment to Queen Elizabeth is in the bad rhythm. (6)

Shakspeare knew that tradition supplies a better fable than any invention can. If he lost any credit of design, he augmented his resources; and, at that day, our petulant demand for originality was not so much pressed. There was no literature for the million. The universal reading, the cheap press, were unknown. A great poet who appears in illiterate times, absorbs into his sphere all the light which is any where radiating. Every intellectual jewel, every flower of sentiment it is his fine office to bring to his people; and he comes to value his memory equally with his invention. (7) He is therefore little solicitous whence his thoughts have been derived; whether through translation, whether through tradition, whether by travel in distant countries, whether by inspiration; from whatever source, they are equally welcome to his uncritical audience. Nay, he borrows very near home. Other men say wise things as well as he; only they say a good many foolish things, and do not know when they have spoken wisely. He knows the sparkle of the true stone, and puts it in high place, wherever he finds it. (8) Such is the happy position of Homer perhaps; of Chaucer, of Saadi. They felt that all wit was their wit. And they are librarians and historiographers, as well as poets. Each romancer was heir and dispenser of all the hundred tales of the world,—

"Presenting Thebes' and Pelops' line
And the tale of Troy divine." (9)

The influence of Chaucer is conspicuous in all our early literature; and more recently not only Pope and Dryden have been beholden to him, but, in the whole society of English writers, a large unacknowledged debt is easily traced. One is charmed with the opulence which feeds so many pensioners. But Chaucer is a huge borrower. Chaucer, it seems, drew continually, through Lydgate and Caxton, from Guido di Colonna, whose Latin romance of the Trojan war was in turn a compilation from Dares Phrygius, Ovid and Statius. Then Petrarch, Boccaccio and the Provençal poets are his benefactors: the Romaunt of the Rose is only judicious translation from William of Lorris and John of Meung: Troilus and Creseide, from Lollius of Urbino: The Cock and the Fox, from the Lais of Marie: The House of Fame, from the French or Italian: and poor Gower he uses as if he were only a brick-kiln or stone-quarry out of which to build his house. (10) He steals by this apology,—that what he takes has no worth where he finds it and the greatest where he leaves it. It has come to be practically a sort of rule in literature, that a man having once shown himself capable of original writing, is entitled thenceforth to steal from the writings of others at discretion. Thought is the property of him who can entertain it and of him who can adequately place it. A certain awkwardness marks the use of borrowed thoughts; but as soon as we have learned what to do with them they become our own.

Thus all originality is relative. Every thinker is retrospective. The learned member of the legislature, at Westminster or at Washington, speaks and votes for thousands. Show us the constituency, and the now invisible channels by which the senator is made aware of their wishes; the crowd of practical and knowing men, who, by correspondence or conversation, are feeding him with evidence, anecdotes and estimates, and it will bereave his fine attitude and resistance of something of their impressiveness. As Sir Robert Peel and Mr. Webster vote, so Locke and Rousseau think, for thousands; and so there were fountains all around Homer, (11) Menu, Saadi, or Milton, from which they drew; friends, lovers, books, traditions, proverbs,—all perished—which, if seen, would go to reduce the wonder. Did the bard speak with authority? Did he feel himself overmatched by any companion? The appeal is to the consciousness of the writer. Is there at last in his breast a Delphi whereof to ask concerning any thought or thing, whether it be verily so, yea or nay? and to have answer, and to rely on that? All the debts which such a man could contract to other wit would never disturb his consciousness of originality; for the ministrations of books and of other minds are a whiff of smoke to that most private reality with which he has conversed. (12)

It is easy to see that what is best written or done by genius in the world, was no man's work, but came by wide social labor, when a thousand wrought like one, sharing the same impulse. Our English Bible is a wonderful specimen of the strength and music of the English language. But it was not made by one man, or at one time; but centuries and churches brought it to perfection. There never was a time when there was not some translation existing. The Liturgy, admired for its energy and pathos, is an anthology of the piety of ages and nations, a translation of the prayers and forms of the Catholic church,—these collected, too, in long periods, from the prayers and meditations of every saint and sacred writer all over the world. (13) Grotius makes the like remark in respect to the Lord's Prayer, that the single clauses of which it is composed were already in use in the time of Christ, in the Rabbinical forms. He picked out the grains of gold. The nervous language of the Common Law, the impressive forms of our courts and the precision and substantial truth of the legal distinctions, are the contribution of all the sharp-sighted, strong-minded men who have lived in the countries where these laws govern. The translation of Plutarch gets its excellence by being translation on translation. There never was a time when there was none. All the truly idiomatic and national phrases are kept, and all others successively picked out and thrown away. Something like the same process had gone on, long before, with the originals of these books. The world takes liberties with world-books. Vedas, Æsop's Fables, Pilpay, Arabian Nights, Cid, Iliad, Robin Hood, Scottish Minstrelsy, are not the work of single men. In the composition of such works the time thinks, the market thinks, the mason, the carpenter, the merchant, the farmer, the fop, all think for us. Every book supplies its time with one good word; every municipal law, every trade, every folly of the day; and the generic catholic genius who is not afraid or ashamed to owe his originality to the originality of all, stands with the next age as the recorder and embodiment of his own. (14)

We have to thank the researches of antiquaries, and the Shakspeare Society, for ascertaining the steps of the English drama, from the Mysteries celebrated in churches and by churchmen, and the final detachment from the church, and the completion of secular plays, from Ferrex and Porrex, (15) and Gammer Gurton's Needle, down to the possession of the stage by the very pieces which Shakspeare altered, remodelled and finally made his own. Elated with success and piqued by the growing interest of the problem, they have left no bookstall unsearched, no chest in a garret unopened, no file of old yellow accounts to decompose in damp and worms, so keen was the hope to discover whether the boy Shakspeare poached or not, whether he held horses at the theatre door, whether he kept school, and why he left in his will only his second-best bed to Ann Hathaway, his wife.

There is somewhat touching in the madness with which the passing age mischooses the object on which all candles shine and all eyes are turned; the care with which it registers every trifle touching Queen Elizabeth and King James, and the Essexes, Leicesters, Burleighs and Buckinghams; and lets pass without a single valuable note the founder of another dynasty, which alone will cause the Tudor dynasty to be remembered,—the man who carries the Saxon race in him by the inspiration which feeds him, and on whose thoughts the foremost people of the world are now for some ages to be nourished, and minds to receive this and not another bias. A popular player;—nobody suspected he was the poet of the human race; and the secret was kept as faithfully from poets and intellectual men as from courtiers and frivolous people. (16) Bacon, who took the inventory of the human understanding for his times, never mentioned his name. Ben Jonson, though we have strained his few words of regard and panegyric, had no suspicion of the elastic fame whose first vibrations he was attempting. He no doubt thought the praise he has conceded to him generous, and esteemed himself, out of all question, the better poet of the two.

If it need wit to know wit, according to the proverb, Shakspeare's time should be capable of recognizing it. Sir Henry Wotton was born four years after Shakspeare, and died twenty-three years after him; and I find, among his correspondents and acquaintances, the following persons: Theodore Beza, Isaac Casaubon, Sir Philip Sidney, the Earl of Essex, Lord Bacon, Sir Walter Raleigh, John Milton, Sir Henry Vane, Isaac Walton, Dr. Donne, Abraham Cowley, Bellarmine, Charles Cotton, John Pym, John Hales, Kepler, Vieta, Albericus Gentilis, Paul Sarpi, Arminius; with all of whom exists some token of his having communicated, without enumerating many others whom doubtless he saw,—Shakspeare, Spenser, Jonson, Beaumont, Massinger, the two Herberts, Marlow, Chapman and the rest. Since the constellation of great men who appeared in Greece in the time of Pericles, there was never any such society;—yet their genius failed them to find out the best head in the universe. (17) Our poet's mask was impenetrable. You cannot see the mountain near. It took a century to make it suspected; and not until two centuries had passed, after his death, did any criticism which we think adequate begin to appear. It was not possible to write the history of Shakspeare till now; for he is the father of German literature: it was with the introduction of Shakspeare into German, by Lessing, and the translation of his works by Wieland and Schlegel, that the rapid burst of German literature was most intimately connected. It was not until the nineteenth century, whose speculative genius is a sort of living Hamlet, that the tragedy of Hamlet could find such wondering readers. (18) Now, literature, philosophy and thought are Shakspearized. His mind is the horizon beyond which, at present, we do not see. Our ears are educated to music by his rhythm. Coleridge and Goethe are the only critics who have expressed our convictions with any adequate fidelity: but there is in all cultivated minds a silent appreciation of his superlative power and beauty, which, like Christianity, qualifies the period.

The Shakspeare Society have inquired in all directions, advertised the missing facts, offered money for any information that will lead to proof,—and with what result? Beside some important illustration of the history of the English stage, to which I have adverted, they have gleaned a few facts touching the property, and dealings in regard to property, of the poet. It appears that from year to year he owned a larger share in the Blackfriars' Theatre: its wardrobe and other appurtenances were his: that he bought an estate in his native village with his earnings as writer and shareholder; that he lived in the best house in Stratford; was intrusted by his neighbors with their commissions in London, as of borrowing money, and the like; that he was a veritable farmer. About the time when he was writing Macbeth, he sues Philip Rogers, in the borough-court of Stratford, for thirty-five shillings, ten pence, for corn delivered to him at different times; and in all respects appears as a good husband, with no reputation for eccentricity or excess. He was a good-natured sort of man, an actor and shareholder in the theatre, not in any striking manner distinguished from other actors and managers. (19) I admit the importance of this information. It was well worth the pains that have been taken to procure it.

But whatever scraps of information concerning his condition these researches may have rescued, they can shed no light upon that infinite invention which is the concealed magnet of his attraction for us. We are very clumsy writers of history. We tell the chronicle of parentage, birth, birth-place, schooling, school-mates, earning of money, marriage, publication of books, celebrity, death; and when we have come to an end of this gossip, no ray of relation appears between it and the goddess-born; and it seems as if, had we dipped at random into the "Modern Plutarch," and read any other life there, it would have fitted the poems as well. (20) It is the essence of poetry to spring, like the rainbow daughter of Wonder, from the invisible, to abolish the past and refuse all history. Malone, Warburton, Dyce and Collier have wasted their oil. The famed theatres, Covent Garden, Drury Lane, the Park and Tremont have vainly assisted. Betterton, Garrick, Kemble, Kean and Macready dedicate their lives to this genius; him they crown, elucidate, obey and express. The genius knows them not. The recitation begins; one golden word leaps out immortal from all this painted pedantry and sweetly torments us with invitations to its own inaccessible homes. I remember I went once to see the Hamlet of a famed performer, the pride of the English stage; and all I then heard and all I now remember of the tragedian was that in which the tragedian had no part; simply Hamlet's question to the ghost:—

"What may this mean,
That thou, dead corse, again in complete steel
Revisit'st thus the glimpses of the moon?"

That imagination which dilates the closet he writes in to the world's dimension, crowds it with agents in rank and order, as quickly reduces the big reality to be the glimpses of the moon. (21) These tricks of his magic spoil for us the illusions of the green-room. Can any biography shed light on the localities into which the Midsummer Night's Dream admits me? Did Shakspeare confide to any notary or parish recorder, sacristan, or surrogate in Stratford, the genesis of that delicate creation? The forest of Arden, the nimble air of Scone Castle, the moonlight of Portia's villa, "the antres vast and desarts idle" of Othello's captivity,—where is the third cousin, or grand-nephew, the chancellor's file of accounts, or private letter, that has kept one word of those transcendent secrets? In fine, in this drama, as in all great works of art,—in the Cyclopæan architecture of Egypt and India, in the Phidian sculpture, the Gothic minsters, the Italian painting, the Ballads of Spain and Scotland,—the Genius draws up the ladder after him, when the creative age goes up to heaven, and gives way to a new age, which sees the works and asks in vain for a history.

Shakspeare is the only biographer of Shakspeare; and even he can tell nothing, except to the Shakspeare in us, that is, to our most apprehensive and sympathetic hour. (22) He cannot step from off his tripod and give us anecdotes of his inspirations. Read the antique documents extricated, analyzed and compared by the assiduous Dyce and Collier, and now read one of these skyey sentences,—aerolites,—which seem to have fallen out of heaven, and which not your experience but the man within the breast has accepted as words of fate, and tell me if they match; if the former account in any manner for the latter; or which gives the most historical insight into the man.

Hence, though our external history is so meagre, yet, with Shakspeare for biographer, instead of Aubrey and Rowe, we have really the information which is material; that which describes character and fortune, that which, if we were about to meet the man and deal with him, would most import us to know. We have his recorded convictions on those questions which knock for answer at every heart,—on life and death, on love, on wealth and poverty, on the prizes of life and the ways whereby we come at them; on the characters of men, and the influences, occult and open, which affect their fortunes; and on those mysterious and demoniacal powers which defy our science and which yet interweave their malice and their gift in our brightest hours. Who ever read the volume of the Sonnets without finding that the poet had there revealed, under masks that are no masks to the intelligent, the lore of friendship and of love; the confusion of sentiments in the most susceptible, and, at the same time, the most intellectual of men? What trait of his private mind has he hidden in his dramas? One can discern, in his ample pictures of the gentleman and the king, what forms and humanities pleased him; his delight in troops of friends, in large hospitality, in cheerful giving. Let Timon, let Warwick, let Antonio the merchant answer for his great heart. So far from Shakspeare's being the least known, he is the one person, in all modern history, known to us. What point of morals, of manners, of economy, of philosophy, of religion, of taste, of the conduct of life, has he not settled? What mystery has he not signified his knowledge of? What office, or function, or district of man's work, has he not remembered? What king has he not taught state, as Talma taught Napoleon? What maiden has not found him finer than her delicacy? What lover has he not outlived? What sage has he not outseen? What gentleman has he not instructed in the rudeness of his behavior?

Some able and appreciating critics think no criticism on Shakspeare valuable that does not rest purely on the dramatic merit; that he is falsely judged as poet and philosopher. I think as highly as these critics of his dramatic merit, but still think it secondary. He was a full man, who liked to talk; a brain exhaling thoughts and images, which, seeking vent, found the drama next at hand. (23) Had he been less, we should have had to consider how well he filled his place, how good a dramatist he was,—and he is the best in the world. But it turns out that what he has to say is of that weight as to withdraw some attention from the vehicle; and he is like some saint whose history is to be rendered into all languages, into verse and prose, into songs and pictures, and cut up into proverbs; so that the occasion which gave the saint's meaning the form of a conversation, or of a prayer, or of a code of laws, is immaterial compared with the universality of its application. So it fares with the wise Shakspeare and his book of life. He wrote the airs for all our modern music: he wrote the text of modern life; the text of manners: he drew the man of England and Europe; the father of the man in America; (24) he drew the man, and described the day, and what is done in it: he read the hearts of men and women, their probity, and their second thought and wiles; the wiles of innocence, and the transitions by which virtues and vices slide into their contraries: he could divide the mother's part from the father's part in the face of the child, or draw the fine demarcations of freedom and of fate: he knew the laws of repression which make the police of nature: and all the sweets and all the terrors of human lot lay in his mind as truly but as softly as the landscape lies on the eye. And the importance of this wisdom of life sinks the form, as of Drama or Epic, out of notice. 'T is like making a question concerning the paper on which a king's message is written.

Shakspeare is as much out of the category of eminent authors, as he is out of the crowd. He is inconceivably wise; the others, conceivably. A good reader can, in a sort, nestle into Plato's brain and think from thence; but not into Shakspeare's. We are still out of doors. For executive faculty, for creation, Shakspeare is unique. No man can imagine it better. He was the farthest reach of subtlety compatible with an individual self,—the subtilest of authors, and only just within the possibility of authorship. (25) With this wisdom of life is the equal endowment of imaginative and of lyric power. He clothed the creatures of his legend with form and sentiments as if they were people who had lived under his roof; and few real men have left such distinct characters as these fictions. And they spoke in language as sweet as it was fit. Yet his talents never seduced him into an ostentation, nor did he harp on one string. An omnipresent humanity co-ordinates all his faculties. Give a man of talents a story to tell, and his partiality will presently appear. He has certain observations, opinions, topics, which have some accidental prominence, and which he disposes all to exhibit. He crams this part and starves that other part, consulting not the fitness of the thing, but his fitness and strength. But Shakspeare has no peculiarity, no importunate topic; but all is duly given; no veins, no curiosities; no cow-painter, no bird-fancier, no mannerist is he: he has no discoverable egotism: the great he tells greatly; the small subordinately. He is wise without emphasis or assertion; he is strong, as nature is strong, who lifts the land into mountain slopes without effort and by the same rule as she floats a bubble in the air, and likes as well to do the one as the other. This makes that equality of power in farce, tragedy, narrative, and love-songs; a merit so incessant that each reader is incredulous of the perception of other readers.

This power of expression, or of transferring the inmost truth of things into music and verse, makes him the type of the poet and has added a new problem to metaphysics. This is that which throws him into natural history, as a main production of the globe, and as announcing new eras and ameliorations. Things were mirrored in his poetry without loss or blur: he could paint the fine with precision, the great with compass, the tragic and the comic indifferently and without any distortion or favor. He carried his powerful execution into minute details, to a hair point; finishes an eyelash or a dimple as firmly as he draws a mountain; and yet these, like nature's, will bear the scrutiny of the solar microscope.

In short, he is the chief example to prove that more or less of production, more or fewer pictures, is a thing indifferent. He had the power to make one picture. Daguerre learned how to let one flower etch its image on his plate of iodine, and then proceeds at leisure to etch a million. There are always objects; but there was never representation. Here is perfect representation, at last; and now let the world of figures sit for their portraits. No recipe can be given for the making of a Shakspeare; but the possibility of the translation of things into song is demonstrated.

His lyric power lies in the genius of the piece. The sonnets, though their excellence is lost in the splendor of the dramas, are as inimitable as they; and it is not a merit of lines, but a total merit of the piece; like the tone of voice of some incomparable person, so is this speech of poetic beings, and any clause as unproducible now as a whole poem.

Though the speeches in the plays, and single lines, have a beauty which tempts the ear to pause on them for their euphuism, yet the sentence is so loaded with meaning and so linked with its foregoers and followers, that the logician is satisfied. His means are as admirable as his ends; every subordinate invention, by which he helps himself to connect some irreconcilable opposites, is a poem too. He is not reduced to dismount and walk because his horses are running off with him in some distant direction: he always rides.
The finest poetry was first experience; but the thought has suffered a transformation since it was an experience. Cultivated men often attain a good degree of skill in writing verses; but it is easy to read, through their poems, their personal history: any one acquainted with the parties can name every figure; this is Andrew and that is Rachel. The sense thus remains prosaic. It is a caterpillar with wings, and not yet a butterfly. In the poet's mind the fact has gone quite over into the new element of thought, and has lost all that is exuvial. This generosity abides with Shakespeare. We say, from the truth and closeness of his pictures, that he knows the lesson by heart. Yet there is not a trace of egotism.

One more royal trait properly belongs to the poet. I mean his cheerfulness, without which no man can be a poet,—for beauty is his aim. He loves virtue, not for its obligation but for its grace: he delights in the world, in man, in woman, for the lovely light that sparkles from them. Beauty, the spirit of joy and hilarity, he sheds over the universe. Epicurus relates that poetry hath such charms that a lover might forsake his mistress to partake of them. And the true bards have been noted for their firm and cheerful temper. Homer lies in sunshine; Chaucer is glad and erect; and Saadi says, "It was rumored abroad that I was penitent; but what had I to do with repentance?" (26) Not less sovereign and cheerful,—much more sovereign and cheerful, is the tone of Shakespeare. His name suggests joy and emancipation to the heart of men. If he should appear in any company of human souls, who would not march in his troop? He touches nothing that does not borrow health and longevity from his festal style.

And now, how stands the account of man with this bard and benefactor, when, in solitude, shutting our ears to the reverberations of his fame, we seek to strike the balance? Solitude has austere lessons; it can teach us to spare both heroes and poets; and it weighs Shakespeare also, and finds him to share the halfness and imperfection of humanity.

Shakespeare, Homer, Dante, Chaucer, saw the splendor of meaning that plays over the visible world; knew that a tree had another use than for apples, and corn another than for meal, and the ball of the earth, than for tillage and roads: that these things bore a second and finer harvest to the mind, being emblems of its thoughts, and conveying in all their natural history a certain mute commentary on human life. (27) Shakespeare employed them as colors to compose his picture. He rested in their beauty; and never took the step which seemed inevitable to such genius, namely to explore the virtue which resides in these symbols and imparts this power:—what is that which they themselves say? He converted the elements which waited on his command, into entertainments. He was master of the revels to mankind. Is it not as if one should have, through majestic powers of science, the comets given into his hand, or the planets and their moons, and should draw them from their orbits to glare with the municipal fireworks on a holiday night, and advertise in all towns, "Very superior pyrotechny this evening"? Are the agents of nature, and the power to understand them, worth no more than a street serenade, or the breath of a cigar? One remembers again the trumpet-text in the Koran,—"The heavens and the earth and all that is between them, think ye we have created them in jest?" As long as the question is of talent and mental power, the world of men has not his equal to show. But when the question is, to life and its materials and its auxiliaries, how does he profit me? What does it signify? It is but a Twelfth Night, or Midsummer-Night's Dream, or Winter Evening's Tale: what signifies another picture more or less? The Egyptian verdict of the Shakespeare Societies comes to mind; that he was a jovial actor and manager. I can not marry this fact to his verse. Other admirable men have led lives in some sort of keeping with their thought; but this man, in wide contrast. Had he been less, had he reached only the common measure of great authors, of Bacon, Milton, Tasso, Cervantes, we might leave the fact in the twilight of human fate: but that this man of men, he who gave to the science of mind a new and larger subject than had ever existed, and planted the standard of humanity some furlongs forward into Chaos,—that he should not be wise for himself;—it must even go into the world's history that the best poet led an obscure and profane life, using his genius for the public amusement. (28)

Well, other men, priest and prophet, Israelite, German and Swede, beheld the same objects: they also saw through them that which was contained. And to what purpose? The beauty straightway vanished; they read commandments, all-excluding mountainous duty; an obligation, a sadness, as of piled mountains, fell on them, and life became ghastly, joyless, a pilgrim's progress, a probation, beleaguered round with doleful histories of Adam's fall and curse behind us; with doomsdays and purgatorial and penal fires before us; and the heart of the seer and the heart of the listener sank in them.

It must be conceded that these are half-views of half-men. The world still wants its poet-priest, a reconciler, who shall not trifle, with Shakespeare the player, nor shall grope in graves, with Swedenborg the mourner; but who shall see, speak, and act, with equal inspiration. For knowledge will brighten the sunshine; right is more beautiful than private affection; and love is compatible with universal wisdom. (29)

Footnotes

Note 1.

This essay was read as a lecture in Exeter Hall, in London, in June, 1848.

Perhaps it is well to bear in mind that Mr. Emerson was reared for the ministry and ordained a clergyman, and that his ancestors for several generations had exercised that office, and moreover that, in New England, up to his day, theatrical representations had been looked at with disfavor by serious and God-fearing people, and the witnessing of such by a minister would, like dancing, have been considered unbecoming indulgence. Although Mr. Emerson emancipated himself from bonds that were merely professional or artificial, he had an inbred distaste for the common amusements of society, feeling that they were unbecoming to a scholar, and that he was not adapted for them, though he was tolerant of them in other people. There was a natural earnestness, and a simple and cheerful asceticism in his early and later life. Yet once in his later life, when he had been induced to go to see Mr. and Mrs. Barney Williams in some bright comedy, he praised their acting and admitted to his daughter that he really much enjoyed theatrical performances, in spite of the feeling that they were not for him. Dancing, for instance, which he considered a proper part of youths' education, would have seemed unbecoming for himself. He says, "It shall be writ in my memoirs ... as it was writ of St. Pachonius, Pes ejus ad saltandum non est commotus omni vita sua." His staying away from theatrical entertainments was instinctive, but he was liberal in the matter and would go to see a real artist. He even went to see the performance of the beautiful dancer Fanny Elssler, although a story which has been too often repeated of his remarks to Margaret Fuller on the subject is as false as it is silly.

In Paris he saw Rachel during the Revolution of 1848, and often told his children of her fierce and splendid declamation of the Marseillaise in the theatre, holding the tricolor aloft. On London in that same year he wrote of seeing Macready in Lear, with Mrs. Butler as Cordelia. It was to see one of Shakspeare's heroes rendered by some master that he went, and probably he never was inside a theatre twenty times in his life, and, so sensitive was he to had taste or ranting, that he was usually sorry that had gone.

The rendering of Richard II. (I cannot remember by whom) more than satisfied him, and he liked to recall the actor's tones in reading this play, an especial favorite of his, to his children. Coriolanus and Julius Cæsar too he enjoyed reading to them, and he selected passages from Shakspeare for them and trained them very carefully for their recitation in school.

He saw Edwin Booth in Boston, and met him later at the house of a friend and had some talk with him. Booth later mentioned with pleasure to their host the fact that Mr. Emerson had not once alluded to his profession or performance in their conversation.

Mr. Emerson once defined the cultivated man as "one who can tell you something new and true about Shakspeare." And he read a good omen for our age in Shakspeare's acceptance: "The book only characterizes the reader. Is Shakspeare the delight of the nineteenth century? That fact only shows whereabouts we are in the ecliptic of the soul."

In writing of Great Men in 1838 in his journal, he says:—

"Swedenborg is scarce yet appreciable. Shakspeare has, for the first time, in our time found adequate criticism, if indeed he have yet found it:—Coleridge, Lamb, Schlegel, Goethe, Very, Herder.

"The great facts of history are four or five names, Homer—Phidias—Jesus—Shakspeare. One or two names more I will not add, but see what these names stand for. All civil history and all philosophy consists of endeavours more or less vain to explain these persons."

In the journal for 1843 he writes: "Plato is weak inasmuch as he is literary. Shakspeare is not literary, but the strong earth itself." Yet from another point of view he writes, "Shakspeare and Plato each sufficed for the culture of a nation."

That Shakspeare and Milton should have been born meant much to him and to mankind. "Who saw Milton, who saw Shakspeare, saw them do their best, and utter their whole heart manlike among their contemporaries."

And again, "No man can be named whose mind still acts on the cultivated intellect of England and America with an energy comparable to that of Milton. As a poet, Shakspeare undoubtedly transcends and far surpasses him in his popularity with foreign nations: but Shakspeare is a voice merely: who and what he was that sang, that sings, we know not."

Note 2.

Mr. Emerson said of Nature:—

No ray is dimmed, no atom worn,
My oldest force is good as new,
And the fresh rose on yonder thorn
Gives back the bending heavens in dew;—

and her cheerful lesson for the artist or poet was that he too could forever re-combine the old material into fresh and splendid pictures. He rejoiced that "the poet is permitted to dip his brush into the old paint-pot with which birds, flowers, the human cheek, the living rock, the broad landscape, the ocean and the eternal sky were painted," and turning from the reading of the plays he says: "'T is Shakspeare's fault that the world appears so empty. He has educated you with his painted world, and this real one seems a huckster's-shop." Again as to his true rendering of men's characters, "I value Shakspeare as a metaphysician and admire the unspoken logic which upholds the structure of Iago, Macbeth, Antony and the rest."

Note 3.

Again the ancient doctrine of the Flowing, and the modern onward and upward stream of Evolution.

Note 4.

The passive Master lent his hand
To the vast soul that o'er him planned.
"The Problem," Poems.

Note 5.

The stage was to Shakspeare his opportunity, as the Lyceum was to Emerson.

Note 6.

Henry VIII., Act V., Scene iv.

Note 7.

This estimate of the value of memory to the poet, typified by the Greeks in their making the Muses the daughters of Mnemosyne, is enlarged upon in the Essay on "Memory" in Natural History of Intellect. Mr. Emerson said once, "Of the most romantic fact the memory is more romantic," and he quotes Quintilian as saying, Quantum ingenii, tantum memoriæ.

Note 8.

In a fragment of verse written in Mr. Emerson's journal of 1831 on the yearning of the poet to enrich himself from the Treasury of the Universe, he says:—

And if to me it is not given
To fetch one ingot thence
Of that unfading gold of Heaven
His merchants may dispense,
Yet well I know the royal mine,

And know the sparkle of its ore,
Know Heaven's truth from lies that shine,—

Explored, they teach us to explore.
"Fragments on the Poet," Poems, Appendix.

Note 9.

Milton, "Il Penseroso."

Note 10.

Taine, in his History of English Literature, thus justifies Chaucer's borrowing or rendering:—

"Chaucer was capable of seeking out, in the old common forest of the middle ages, stories and legends, to replant them in his own soil and make them send out new shoots.... He has the right and power of copying and translating because by dint of retouching he impresses ... his original mark. He re-creates what he imitates.... At the distance of a century and a half he has affinity with the poets of Elizabeth by his gallery of pictures."

The dates of Lydgate and Caxton show a mistake as to his use of them. Caxton, following Chaucer, when he introduced the printing-press to England, printed his poems and those of Lydgate, who was younger than Chaucer. In his House of Fame, Chaucer places, in his vision, "on a pillar higher than the rest, Homer and Livy, Dares the Phrygian, Guido Colonna, Geoffrey of Monmouth and the other historians of the war of Troy" [Taine's History of English Literature], a due recognition of his debt for Troylus and Cryseyde. As for Gower, he was Chaucer's exact contemporary and friend, and Chaucer dedicated this poem to him.

Note 11.

Kipling irreverently tells of Homer's borrowings thus:—

"When 'Omer smote 'is bloomin' lyre,
He 'd 'eard men sing by land an' sea;
An' what he thought 'e might require,
'E went an' took—the same as me!"
And says of his humble audience:—

"They knew 'e stole; 'e knew they knowed.
They did n't tell, nor make a fuss,
But winked at 'Omer down the road,
An' 'e winked back—the same as us!"

Note 12.

Dr. Holmes's remark with regard to the preceding page is: "The reason why Emerson has so much to say on this subject of borrowing, especially when treating of Plato and Shakspeare, is obvious enough. He was arguing his own cause—not defending himself," etc. In Letters and Social Aims, Mr. Emerson discusses Quotation and Originality.

Note 13.

Mr. Emerson had tender associations with the Book of Common Prayer. His mother had been brought up in the Episcopal communion, and the prayer-book of her youth was always by her, though after her marriage she attended her husband's church. [In Mr. Cabot's Memoir, vol. ii. p. 572, see Mr. Emerson's letter on his mother's death.]

Note 14.

Landor says of these borrowings of Shakspeare, "He breathed upon dead bodies and brought them to life."

Note 15.

The princes Ferrex and Porrex, brothers and rivals for the ancient British throne, are characters in the tragedy Gorboduc by Norton and Sackville, to which the date 1561 is assigned. Gammer Gurton's Needle is a comedy of the same period.

Note 16.

Journal, 1864. "Shakspeare puts us all out. No theory will account for him. He neglected his works, perchance he did not know their value? Ay, but he did; witness the sonnets. He went into company as a listener, hiding himself, [Greek]; was only remembered by all as a delightful companion."

Note 17.

England's genius filled all measure
Of heart and soul, of strength and pleasure,
Gave to the mind its emperor,
And life was larger than before:
Nor sequent centuries could hit
Orbit and sum of Shakspeare's wit.
The men who lived with him became
Poets, for the air was fame.
"The Solution," Poems.

Note 18.

While writing this, Mr. Emerson was surrounded by persons paralyzed for active life in the common world by the doubts of conscience or entangled in over-fine-spun webs of their intellect. [back]

Note 19.

Journal, 1837. "I either read or inferred to-day in the Westminster Review that Shakspeare was not a popular man in his day. How true and wise. He sat alone and walked alone, a visionary poet, and came with his piece, modest but discerning, to the players, and was too glad to get it received, whilst he was too superior not to see its transcendent claims."

Note 20.

The following is the "Exordium of a lecture on Poetry and Eloquence," given in London in 1848:

"Shakspeare is nothing but a large utterance. We cannot find that anything in his age was more worth telling than anything in ours; nor give any account of his existence, but only the fact that there was a wonderful symbolizer and expresser, who has no rival in the ages, and who has thrown an accidental lustre over his time and subject."

In the lecture on "Works and Days" he wrote, "Shakspeare made his Hamlet as a bird weaves its nest." And in that on "Inspiration" in Letters and Social Aims: "Shakspeare seems to you miraculous, but the wonderful juxtapositions, parallelisms, transfers, which his genius effected, were all to him locked together as links of a chain, and the mode precisely as conceivable and familiar to higher intelligence as the index-making of the literary hack."

Journal, 1838. "Read Lear yesterday and Hamlet to-day with new wonder and mused much on the great Soul in the broad continuous daylight of these poems. Especially I wonder at the perfect reception this wit and immense knowledge of life and intellectual superiority find in us all in connection with our utter incapacity to produce anything like it. The superior tone of Hamlet in all the conversations how perfectly preserved, without any mediocrity, much less any dulness in the other speakers.

"How real the loftiness! an inborn gentleman; and above that, an exalted intellect. What incessant growth and plenitude of thought,—pausing on itself never an instant, and each sally of wit sufficient to save the play. How true then and unerring the earnest of the dialogue, as when Hamlet talks with the Queen. How terrible his discourse! What less can be said of the perfect mastery, as by a superior being, of the conduct of the drama, as the free introduction of this capital advice to the players; the commanding good sense which never retreats except before the Godhead which inspires certain passages—the more I think of it, the more I wonder. I will think nothing impossible to man. No Parthenon, no sculpture, no picture, no architecture can be named beside this. All this is perfectly visible to me and to many,—the wonderful truth and mastery of this work, of these works,—yet for our lives could not I, or any man, or all men, produce anything comparable to one scene in Hamlet or Lear. With all my admiration of this life-like picture, set me to producing a match for it, and I should instantly depart into mouthing rhetoric.... One other fact Shakspeare presents us; that not by books are great poets made. Somewhat—and much, he unquestionably owes to his books; but you could not find in his circumstances the history of his poems. It was made without hands in his invisible world. A mightier magic than any learning, the deep logic of cause and effect he studied: its roots were cast so deep, therefore it flung out its branches so high."

Note 21.

Mr. Edwin P. Whipple, writing in Harper's Monthly in 1882, relates how in a long drive with Mr. Emerson, after a lecture, "The conversation at last drifted to contemporary actors who assumed to personate leading characters in Shakspeare's greatest plays. Had I ever seen an actor who satisfied me when he pretended to be Hamlet or Othello, Lear or Macbeth? Yes, I had seen the elder Booth in these characters. Though not perfect, he approached nearer to perfection than any other actor I knew—

"'Ah,' said Emerson, [after] the three minutes I consumed in eulogizing Booth,... 'I see you are one of the happy mortals who are capable of being carried away by an actor of Shakspeare. Now, whenever I visit the theatre to witness the performance of one of his dramas, I am carried away by the poet. I went last Tuesday to see Macready in Hamlet. I got along very well until he came to the passage:—

"'thou, dead corse, again, in complete steel,
Revisit'st thus the glimpses of the moon:"—

and then actor, theatre, all vanished in view of that solving and dissolving imagination, which could reduce this big globe and all it inherits into mere "glimpses of the moon." The play went on, but, absorbed in this one thought of the mighty master, I paid no heed to it.'

"What specially impressed me, as Emerson was speaking, was his glance at our surroundings as he slowly uttered, 'glimpses of the moon,' for here above us was the same moon which must have given birth to Shakspeare's thought.... Afterward, in his lecture on Shakspeare, Emerson made use of the thought suggested in our ride by moonlight. He said, 'That imagination which dilates the closet he writes in to the world's dimensions, crowds it with agents in rank and order, as quickly reduces the big reality to be the "glimpses of the moon."'... In the printed lecture, there is one sentence declaring the absolute insufficiency of any actor, in any theatre, to fix attention on himself while uttering Shakspeare's words, which seems to me the most exquisite statement ever made of the magical suggestiveness of Shakspeare's expression. I have often quoted it, but it will bear quotation again and again, as the best prose sentence ever written on this side of the Atlantic: 'The recitation begins; one golden word leaps out immortal from all this painted pedantry, and sweetly torments us with invitations to its own inaccessible homes.'"

Note 22.

The little Shakspeare in the maiden's heart
Makes Romeo of a ploughboy on his cart;
Opens the eye to Virtue's starlike meed
And gives persuasion to a gentle deed.
"The Enchanter," Poems, Appendix.

Note 23.

And yet perhaps there is some truth in Dr. Richard Garnett's word in his Life of Emerson:

"Emerson is incapable of contemplating Shakspeare with the eye of a dramatic critic."

Just after Mr. Emerson settled in Concord he read with great pleasure Henry Taylor's play Philip van Artevelde, then recently published. He wrote in his journal for 1835:—

"I think Taylor's poem is the best light we have ever had upon the genius of Shakspeare. We have made a miracle of Shakspeare, a haze of light instead of a guiding torch, by accepting unquestioned all the tavern stories about his want of education, and total unconsciousness. The internal evidence all the time is irresistible that he was no such person. He was a man, like this Taylor, of strong sense and of great cultivation; an excellent Latin scholar, and of extensive and select reading, so as to have formed his theories of many historical characters with as much clearness as Gibbon or Niebuhr or Goethe. He wrote for intelligent persons, and wrote with intention. He had Taylor's strong good sense, and added to it his own wonderful facility of execution which aerates and sublimes all language the moment he uses it, or more truly, animates every word."

Note 24.

Lowell, in one of his essays, calls attention to the survival in New England of the type of face of the English in Queen Elizabeth's day even more than in the mother country, and also to the old English expressions, obsolete in England, but still current on New England farms.

Note 25.

Journal, 1838. fills us with wonder the first time we approach him. We go away, and work and think, for years, and come again,—he astonishes us anew. Then, having drank deeply and saturated us with his genius, we lose sight of him for another period of years. By and by we return, and there he stands immeasurable as at first. We have grown wiser, but only that we should see him wiser than ever. He resembles a high mountain which the traveller sees in the morning, and thinks he shall quickly near it and pass it, and leave it behind. But he journeys all day till noon, till night. There still is the dim mountain close by him, having scarce altered its bearings since the morning light."

Note 26.

And yet it seemeth not to me
That the high gods love tragedy;
For Saadi sat in the sun,
And thanks was his contrition;

And yet his runes he rightly read,

And to his folk his message sped.
"Saadi," Poems.

Note 27.

This image appears in "The Apology" in the Poems.

Note 28.

The Puritan shrinking from the form in which the great poet embodied his thought or oracles or dreams still appears in the journal of 1852, yet, contrasted to the dismal seers, Shakspeare is well-nigh pardoned his levity.

"There was never anything more excellent came from a human brain than the plays of Shakspeare, bating only that they were plays. The Greek has a real advantage of them in the degree in which his dramas had a religious office. Could the priest look him in the face without blenching?"

In 1839 Mr. Emerson had written:—

"It is in the nature of things that the highest originality must be moral. The only person who can be entirely independent of this fountain of literature and equal to it, must be a prophet in his own proper person. Shakspeare, the first literary genius of the world, leans on the Bible: his poetry supposes it. If we examine this brilliant influence, Shakspeare, as it lies in our minds, we shall find it reverent, deeply indebted to the traditional morality, in short, compared with the tone of the prophets, Secondary. On the other hand, the Prophets do not imply the existence of Shakspeare or Homer,—to no books or arts,—only to dread Ideas and emotions."

Note 29.

All through his life Mr. Emerson felt increasing thankfulness for "the Spirit of joy which Shakspeare had shed over the Universe." In 1864 he wrote:—

"When I read Shakspeare, as lately, I think the criticism and study of him to be in their infancy. The wonder grows of his long obscurity:—how could you hide the only man that ever wrote from all men who delight in reading?"

And again he wrote: "Your criticism is profane. Shakspeare by Shakspeare. The poet in his interlunation is a critic,"—that is, his worst is criticised by his best performance.

Journal, 1864. "How to say it I know not, but I know that the point of praise of Shakspeare is the pure poetic power: he is the chosen closet companion, who can, at any moment, by incessant surprises, work the miracle of mythologizing every fact of the common life; as snow, or moonlight, or the level rays of sunrise lend a momentary glow to Pump and wood-pile."

And again: 1836. "It is easy to solve the problem of individual existence. Why Milton, Shakspeare, or Canova should be there is reason enough. But why the million should exist drunk with the opium of Time and Custom does not appear."

But even Shakspeare must not be idolized. The soul must rely on itself, that is, on the universal fountain of beauty, wisdom and goodness to which it is open. So thus he draws the moral:—

1838. "The indisposition of men to go back to the source and mix with Deity is the reason of degradation and decay. Education is expended in the measurement and imitation of effects in the study of Shakspeare, for example, as itself a perfect being—instead of using Shakspeare merely as an effect of which the cause is with every scholar. Thus the college becomes idolatrous—a temple full of idols. Shakspeare will never be made by the study of Shakspeare. I know not how directions for greatness can be given, yet greatness may be inspired."

Feb. 1838. "Consider too how Shakspeare and Milton are formed. They are just such men as we all are to contemporaries, and none suspected their superiority,—but after all were dead, and a generation or two besides, it is discovered that they surpass all. Each of us then take the same moral to himself."

William Shakespeare – A Tribute in Verse

Index of Contents
To the Memory of My Beloved, the Author, Mr William Shakespeare, & What He Hath Left Us by Ben Jonson
Shakespeare by Matthew Arnold
An Epitaph On The Admirable Dramatic Poet W. Shakespeare by John Milton
Shakespeare by Henry Wadsworth Longfellow
Elegy On Mr. William Shakespeare by William Basse
Shakespeare by Vachel Lindsay
The Spirit of Shakespeare by George Meredith
To Shakespeare by Lord Alfred Douglas
To Shakespeare (I) by Frances Anne Kemble
To Shakespeare (II) by Frances Anne Kemble
To Shakespeare (III) by Frances Anne Kemble
Shakespeare and Milton by Walter Savage Landor
A Shakespeare Memorial by Alfred Austin
Shakespeare by Mathilde Blind
Shakespeare by Robert Crawford
Shakespeare by Thomas Gent
Shakespeare's Mourners by John Bannister Tabb
Shakespeare by Philip Henry Savage
Shakespeare by Lucretia Maria Davidson
Shakespeare by Frederick George Scott
Shakespeare's Kingdom by Alfred Noyes
Shakespeare 1916 by Sir Ronald Ross
Song, In Imitation of Shakspeare's by James Beattie
In A Letter To C. P. Esq. In Imitation o Shakspeare by William Cowper
Shakspeare. (An Ode For His Three-Hundredth Birthday) by Martin Farquhar Tupper
On The Site of A Mulberry-Tree; Planted By Wm. Shakspeare; Felled By The Rev. F. Gastrell by Dante Gabriel Rossetti

To The Memory of My Beloved, The Author, Mr William Shakespeare, And What He Hath Left Us by Ben Jonson

To draw no envy, Shakespeare, on thy name
Am I thus ample to thy book and fame;
While I confess thy writings to be such
As neither Man nor Muse can praise too much.
'Tis true, and all men's suffrage. But these ways
Were not the paths I meant unto thy praise;
For silliest ignorance on these may light,
Which when it sounds at best but echoes right;
Or blind affection, which doth ne'er advance
The truth, but gropes, and urges all by chance;
Or crafty malice might pretend this praise,
And think to ruin where it seemed to raise.
These are as some infamous bawd or whore
Should praise a matron. What could hurt her more?
But thou art proof against them, and indeed
Above th' ill fortune of them, or the need.
I therefore will begin: Soul of the Age!
The applause, delight, the wonder of our stage!
My Shakespeare, rise; I will not lodge thee by
Chaucer, or Spenser, or bid Beaumont lie
A little further, to make thee a room:
Thou art a monument without a tomb,
And art alive still, while thy book doth live,
And we have wits to read, and praise to give.
That I not mix thee so, my brain excuses,
I mean with great but disproportioned Muses,
For if I thought my judgement were of years,
I should commit thee surely with thy peers,
And tell how far thou didst our Lyly outshine,
Or sporting Kyd, or Marlowe's mighty line.
And though thou hadst small Latin and less Greek,
From thence to honour thee I would not seek
For names; but call forth thundering Aeschylus,
Euripides, and Sophocles to us,
Pacuvius, Accius, him of Cordova dead,
To live again, to hear thy buskin tread,
And shake a stage; or, when thy socks were on,
Leave thee alone for the comparison
Of all that insolent Greece or haughty Rome
Sent forth, or since did from their ashes come.
Triumph, my Britain, thou hast one to show
To whom all scenes of Europe homage owe.
He was not of an age, but for all time!
And all the Muses still were in their prime
When, like Apollo, he came forth to warm
Our ears, or, like a Mercury, to charm!
Nature herself was proud of his designs,
And joyed to wear the dressing of his lines!
Which were so richly spun, and woven so fit,
As, since, she will vouchsafe no other wit.
The merry Greek, tart Aristophanes,

Neat Terence, witty Plautus, now not please;
But antiquated and deserted lie,
As they were not of Nature's family.
Yet must I not give Nature all; thy art,
My gentle Shakespeare, must enjoy a part.
For though the poet's matter nature be,
His art doth give the fashion; and that he
Who casts to write a living line must sweat
(Such as thine are) and strike the second heat
Upon the Muses' anvil; turn the same,
And himself with it, that he thinks to frame,
Or for the laurel he may gain a scorn;
For a good poet's made as well as born.
And such wert thou. Look how the father's face
Lives in his issue, even so the race
Of Shakespeare's mind and manners brightly shines
In his well turned and true-filed lines:
In each of which he seems to shake a lance,
As brandished at the eyes of ignorance.
Sweet swan of Avon! what a sight it were
To see thee in our waters yet appear,
And make those flights upon the banks of Thames,
That did so take Eliza and our James!
But stay, I see thee in the hemisphere
Advanced, and made a constellation there:
Shine forth, thou Star of Poets, and with rage,
Or influence, chide or cheer the drooping stage,
Which, since thy flight from hence, hath mourned like night,
And despairs day, but for thy volume's light.

Shakespeare by Matthew Arnold

Others abide our question. Thou art free.
We ask and ask—Thou smilest and art still,
Out-topping knowledge. For the loftiest hill,
Who to the stars uncrowns his majesty,

Planting his steadfast footsteps in the sea,
Making the heaven of heavens his dwelling-place,
Spares but the cloudy border of his base
To the foil'd searching of mortality;

And thou, who didst the stars and sunbeams know,
Self-school'd, self-scann'd, self-honour'd, self-secure,
Didst tread on earth unguess'd at.—Better so!

All pains the immortal spirit must endure,
All weakness which impairs, all griefs which bow,
Find their sole speech in that victorious brow

An Epitaph On The Admirable Dramatic Poet W. Shakespeare by John Milton

What needs my Shakespeare for his honored bones
The labor of an age in piled stones?
Or that his hallowed reliques should be hid
Under a star-ypointing pyramid?
Dear son of Memory, great heir of Fame,
What need'st thou such weak witness of thy name?
Thou in our wonder and astonishment
Hast built thy self a livelong monument.
For whilst, to th' shame of slow-endeavoring art,
Thy easy numbers flow, and that each heart
Hath from the leaves of thy unvalued book
Those Delphic lines with deep impression took,
Then thou, our fancy of itself bereaving,
Dost make us marble with too much conceiving,
And so sepulchred in such pomp dost lie
That kings for such a tomb would wish to die.

Shakespeare by Henry Wadsworth Longfellow

A vision as of crowded city streets,
With human life in endless overflow;
Thunder of thoroughfares; trumpets that blow
To battle; clamor, in obscure retreats,
Of sailors landed from their anchored fleets;
Tolling of bells in turrets, and below
Voices of children, and bright flowers that throw
O'er garden-walls their intermingled sweets!
This vision comes to me when I unfold
The volume of the Poet paramount,
Whom all the Muses loved, not one alone;—
Into his hands they put the lyre of gold,
And, crowned with sacred laurel at their fount,
Placed him as Musagetes on their throne.

Elegy On Mr. William Shakespeare by William Basse

Renowned Spenser, lie a thought more nigh
To learned Chaucer, and rare Beaumont lie
A little nearer Spenser, to make room
For Shakespeare in your threefold, fourfold tomb.
To lodge all four in one bed, make a shift
Until Doomsday, for hardly will a fift

Betwixt this day and that by Fate be slain,
For whom your curtains may be drawn again.
If your precedency in death doth bar
A fourth place in your sacred sepulchre,
Under this carved marble of thine own,
Sleep, rare tragedian, Shakespeare, sleep alone;
Thy unmolested peace, unshared cave
Possess as lord, not tenant of thy grave,
That unto us and others it may be
Honour hereafter to be laid by thee.

Shakespeare by Vachel Lindsay

Would that in body and spirit Shakespeare came
Visible emperor of the deeds of Time,
With Justice still the genius of his rhyme,
Giving each man his due, each passion grace,
Impartial as the rain from Heaven's face
Or sunshine from the heaven-enthroned sun.
Sweet Swan of Avon, come to us again.
Teach us to write, and writing, to be men.

The Spirit of Shakespeare by George Meredith

Thy greatest knew thee, Mother Earth; unsoured
He knew thy sons. He probed from hell to hell
Of human passions, but of love deflowered
His wisdom was not, for he knew thee well.
Thence came the honeyed corner at his lips,
The conquering smile wherein his spirit sails
Calm as the God who the white sea-wave whips,
Yet full of speech and intershifting tales,
Close mirrors of us: thence had he the laugh
We feel is thine: broad as ten thousand beeves
At pasture! thence thy songs, that winnow chaff
From grain, bid sick Philosophy's last leaves
Whirl, if they have no response-they enforced
To fatten Earth when from her soul divorced.

To Shakespeare by Lord Alfred Douglas

Most tuneful singer, lover tenderest,
Most sad, most piteous, and most musical,
Thine is the shrine more pilgrim-worn than all
The shrines of singers; high above the rest

Thy trumpet sounds most loud, most manifest.
Yet better were it if a lonely call
Of woodland birds, a song, a madrigal,
Were all the jetsam of thy sea's unrest.

For now thy praises have become too loud
On vulgar lips, and every yelping cur
Yaps thee a paean; the whiles little men,
Not tall enough to worship in a crowd,
Spit their small wits at thee. Ah! better then
The broken shrine, the lonely worshipper.

To Shakespeare (I) by Frances Anne Kemble

If from the height of that celestial sphere
Where now thou dwell'st, spirit powerful and sweet!
Thou yet canst love the race that sojourn here,
How must thou joy, with pleasure not unmeet
For thy exalted state, to know how dear
Thy memory is held throughout the earth,
Beyond the favoured land that gave thee birth.
E'en in thy seat in Heaven, thou may'st receive
Thanks, praise, and love, and wonder ever new,
From human hearts, who in thy verse perceive
All that humanity calls good and true;
Nor dost thou for each mortal blemish grieve,
They from thy glorious works have fall'n away,
As from thy soul its outward form of clay.

To Shakespeare (II) by Frances Anne Kemble

Oft, when my lips I open to rehearse
Thy wondrous spells of wisdom and of power,
And that my voice and thy immortal verse
On listening ears and hearts I mingled pour,
I shrink dismayed—and awful doth appear
The vain presumption of my own weak deed;
Thy glorious spirit seems to mine so near,
That suddenly I tremble as I read—
Thee an invisible auditor I fear:
Oh, if it might be so, my master dear!
With what beseeching would I pray to thee,
To make me equal to my noble task,
Succour from thee, how humbly would I ask,
Thy worthiest works to utter worthily.

To Shakespeare (III) by Frances Anne Kemble

Shelter and succour such as common men
Afford the weaker partners of their fate,
Have I derived from thee—from thee, most great
And powerful genius! whose sublime control,
Still from thy grave governs each human soul,
That reads the wondrous records of thy pen.
From sordid sorrows thou hast set me free,
And turned from want's grim ways my tottering feet,
And to sad empty hours, given royally,
A labour, than all leisure far more sweet:
The daily bread, for which we humbly pray,
Thou gavest me as if I were thy child,
And still with converse noble, wise, and mild,
Charmed from despair my sinking soul away;
Shall I not bless the need, to which was given
Of all the angels in the host of heaven,
Thee, for my guardian, spirit strong and bland!
Lord of the speech of my dear native land!

Shakespeare and Milton by Walter Savage Landor

The tongue of England, that which myriads
Have spoken and will speak, were paralyz'd
Hereafter, but two mighty men stand forth
Above the flight of ages, two alone;
One crying out,
All nations spoke through me.
The other:
True; and through this trumpet burst God's word;
The fall of Angels, and the doom
First of immortal, then of mortal, Man.
Glory! be glory! not to me, to God.

A Shakespeare Memorial by Alfred Austin

Why should we lodge in marble or in bronze
Spirits more vast than earth, or sea, or sky?
Wiser the silent worshipper that cons
Their words for wisdom that will never die.
Unto the favourite of the passing hour
Erect the statue and parade the bust;
Whereon decisive Time will slowly shower
Oblivion's refuse and disdainful dust.
The Monarchs of the Mind, self-sceptred Kings,

Need no memento to transmit their name:
Throned on their thoughts and high imaginings,
They are the Lords, not sycophants of Fame.
Raise pedestals to perishable stuff:
Gods for themselves are monuments enough.

Shakespeare by Mathilde Blind

Yearning to know herself for all she was,
Her passionate clash of warring good and ill,
Her new life ever ground in Death's old mill,
With every delicate detail and en masse,—
Blind Nature strove. Lo, then it came to pass,
That Time, to work out her unconscious Will,
Once wrought the Mind which she had groped for still,
And she beheld herself as in a glass.

The world of men, unrolled before our sight,
Showed like a map, where stream and waterfall
And village-cradling vale and cloud-capped height
Stand faithfully recorded, great and small;
For Shakespeare was, and at his touch, with light
Impartial as the Sun's, revealed the All.

Shakespeare by Robert Crawford

And what think ye of Shakespeare? 'Twas not he
Of Stratford is the lord of England's lyre;
Ay, not the rustic lad, whoe'er it be,
Momentous in his doing and desire.
But little Latin and less Greek? Ah, no!
It was a teeming scholar who enwrought
The wondrous pages where the wisest go
For th' culmination of the life of thought.
No jovial actor, no mere Shakescene who
Found it so hard his dear name to indite,
The marvellous pictures of our nature drew
And limned the universe in his delight.
We do not know the man; but 'twas not Will
Whose hand is on the lyre of England still.

Shakespeare by Thomas Gent

While o'er this pageant of sublunar things
Oblivion spreads her unrelenting wings,

And sweeps adown her dark unebbing tide
Man, and his mightiest monuments of pride-
Alone, aloft, immutable, sublime,
Star-like, ensphered above the track of time,
Great SHAKSPEARE beams with undiminish'd ray.
His bright creations sacred from decay,
Like Nature's self, whose living form he drew,
Though still the same, still beautiful and new.

He came, untaught in academic bowers,
A gift to Glory from the Sylvan powers:
But what keen Sage, with all the science fraught,
By elder bards or later critics taught,
Shall count the cords of his mellifluous shell,
Span the vast fabric of his fame, and tell
By what strange arts he bade the structure rise-
On what deep site the strong foundation lies?
This, why should scholiasts labour to reveal?
We all can answer it, we all can feel,
Ten thousand sympathies, attesting, start-
For SHAKSPEARE'S Temple, is the human heart!

Lord of a throne which mortal ne'er shall share-
Despot adored! he rales and revels there.
Who but has found, where'er his track hath been,
Through life's oft shifting, multifarious scene,
Still at his side the genial Bard attend,
His loved companion, counsellor, and friend!

The Thespian Sisters nurtured in the schools
Of Greece and Rome, and long coerced by rules,
Scarce moved the inmates of their native hearth
With tiny pathos and with trivial mirth,
Till She, great muse of daring enterprise,
Delighted ENGLAND! saw her SHAKSPEARE rise!

Then, first aroused in that appointed hour,
The Tragic Muse confess'd th' inspiring power;
Sudden before the startled earth she stood,
A giant spectre, weeping tears and blood;
Guilt shrunk appall'd, Despair embraced his shroud,
And Terror shriek'd, and Pity sobb'd aloud;-
Then, first Thalia with dilated ken
And quicken'd footstep pierced the walks of men;
Then Folly blush'd, Vice fled the general hiss,
Delight met Reason with a loving kiss;
At Satire's glance Pride smooth'd his low'ring crest,
The Graces weaved the dance.-And last and best
Came Momus down in Falstaff's form to earth.
To make the world one universe of mirth!

Such Sympathies the glorious Bard endear!
Thus fair he walks in Man's diurnal sphere.
But when, upborne on bright Invention's wings.
He dares the realms of uncreated things,
Forms more divine, more dreadful, start to view,
Than ever Hades or Olympus knew.
Round the dark cauldron, terrible and fell,
The midnight Witches breathe the songs of hell;
Delighted Ariel wings his fiery way
To whirl the storm, the wheeling Orbs to stay;
Then bathes in honey-dews, and sleeps in flowers;
Meanwhile, young Oberon, girt with shadowy powers,
Pursues o'er Ocean's verge the pale cold Moon,
Or hymns her, riding in her highest noon.

Thus graced, thus glorified, shall SHAKSPEARE crave
The Sculptor's skill, the pageant of the grave?
HE needs it not-but Gratitude demands
This votive offering at his Country's hands.
Haply, e'er now, from blissful bowers on high,
From some Parnassus of the empyreal sky,
Pleased, o'er this dome the gentle Spirit bends,
Accepts the gift, and hails us as his friends-
Yet smiles, perchance, to think when envious Time
O'er Bust and Urn shall bid his ivies climb,
When Palaces and Pyramids shall fall-
HIS PAGE SHALL TRIUMPH-still surviving all-
'Till Earth itself, 'like breath upon the wind,'
Shall melt away, 'nor leave a rack behind!'

Shakespeare's Mourners by John Bannister Tabb

I saw the grave of Shakespeare in a dream,
And round about it grouped a wondrous throng,
His own majestic mourners, who belong
Forever to the Stage of Life, and seem
The rivals of reality. Supreme
Stood Hamlet, as erewhile the graves among,
Mantled in thought: and sad Ophelia sung
The same swan-dirge she chanted in the stream.
Othello, dark in destiny's eclipse,
Laid on the tomb a lily. Near him wept
Dejected Constance. Fair Cordelia's lips
Moved prayerfully the while her father slept,
And each and all, inspired of vital breath,
Kept vigil o'er the sacred spoils of death.

Shakespeare by Philip Henry Savage

Through time untimed, if truly great, a Name
Reverence compels and, that forgotten, shame.
But in the stress of living you shall scan,
Yea, touch and censure, great or small, the Man.

Shakespeare by Lucretia Maria Davidson

Shakspeare!' with all thy faults, (and few have more,)
I love thee still,' and still will con thee o'er.
Heaven, in compassion to man's erring heart,
Gave thee of virtue — then, of vice a part,
Lest we, in wonder here, should bow before thee,
Break God's commandment, worship, and adore thee:
But admiration now, and sorrow join;
His works we reverence, while we pity thine.

Shakespeare by Frederick George Scott

Unseen in the great minister dome of time,
Whose shafts are centuries, its spangled roof
The vaulted universe, our master sits,
And organ-voices like a far-off chime
Roll thro' the aisles of thought. The sunlight flits

From arch to arch, and, as he sits aloof,
Kings, heroes, priests, in concourse vast, sublime,
Glances of love and cries from battle-field,
His wizard power breathes on the living air.
Warm faces gleam and pass, child, woman, man,

In the long multitude; but he, concealed,
Our bard eludes us, vainly each face we scan,
It is not he; his features are not there;
But, being thus hid, his greatness is revealed.

Shakespeare's Kingdom by Alfred Noyes

When Shakespeare came to London
He met no shouting throngs;
He carried in his knapsack
A scroll of quiet songs.

No proud heraldic trumpet

Acclaimed him on his way;
Their court and camp have perished;
The songs live on for ay.

Nobody saw or heard them,
But, all around him there,
Spirits of light and music
Went treading the April air.

He passed like any pedlar,
Yet he had wealth untold.
The galleons of th' armada
Could not contain his gold.

The kings rode on to darkness.
In England's conquering hour,
Unseen arrived her splendour;
Unknown, her conquering power.

Shakespeare 1916 by Sir Ronald Ross

Now when the sinking Sun reeketh with blood,
And the gore-gushing vapors rent by him
Rend him and bury him: now the World is dim
As when great thunders gather for the flood,
And in the darkness men die where they stood,
And dying slay, or scatter'd limb from limb
Cease in a flash where mad-eyed cherubim
Of Death destroy them in the night and mud:
When landmarks vanish—murder is become
A glory—cowardice, conscience— and to lie,
A law—to govern, but to serve a time:—
We dying, lifting bloodied eyes and dumb,
Behold the silver star serene on high,
That is thy spirit there, O Master Mind sublime.

Song, In Imitation of Shakspeare's by James Beattie

I
Blow, blow, thou vernal gale!
Thy balm will not avail
To ease my aching breast;
Though thou the billows smooth,
Thy murmurs cannot soothe
My weary soul to rest.

II

Flow, flow, thou tuneful stream!
Infuse the easy dream
Into the peaceful soul;
But thou canst not compose
The tumult of my woes,
Though soft thy waters roll.

III
Blush, blush, ye fairest flowers!
Beauties surpassing yours
My Rosalind adorn;
Nor is the Winter's blast,
That lays your glories waste,
So killing as her scorn.

IV
Breathe, breathe, ye tender lays,
That linger down the maze
Of yonder winding grove;
O let your soft control
Bend her relenting soul
To pity and to love.

V
Fade, fade, ye flowerets fair!
Gales, fan no more the air!
Ye streams, forget to glide;
Be hush'd each vernal strain;
Since nought can soothe my pain,
Nor mitigate her pride.

In A Letter To C. P. Esq. In Imitation Of Shakspeare by William Cowper

Trust me the meed of praise, dealt thriftily
From the nice scale of judgement, honours more
Than does the lavish and o'erbearing tide
Of profuse courtesy. Not all the gems
Of India's richest soil at random spread
O'er the gay vesture of some glittering dame,
Give such alluring vantage to the person,
As the scant lustre of a few, with choice
And comely guise of ornament disposed.

Shakspeare. (An Ode For His Three-Hundredth Birthday) by Martin Farquhar Tupper

I.
Immortal! risen to thy Rest,

Immortal! throned among the Blest,
Immortal! long an heir sublime
Of realms outreaching space and time,—
How shall we dare, or hope, to raise
A fitting homage of high praise
To please thy Spirit, sphered on high
Where planets roll and comets fly?
How may not thy pure fame be marr'd
By the damp breath of earthly bard,
Presuming in his zeal too bold
To gild the bright refinèd gold?
Or how canst thou, fill'd with God's love,
And tranced among the saints above,
Endure that men should seem and be
Idolaters in praise of thee!
Forgive our love, forgive our zeal,—
We cannot guess how spirits feel;
And may our homage offered thus
Please HIM who made both thee, and us!

II.
Immortal also on this darker Earth
As in those brighter spheres,
Now will we consecrate our Shakespeare's birth,
This day three hundred years!
And so from age to age for evermore
His glory shall extend,
With men of every land the wide world o'er,
Till Time itself shall end!
For, he is our's; and well with pride and joy
England may bless her son,
The Stratford scholar and the Warwick boy
That every crown hath won!
Let others boast their wisest and their best,
To each a prize may fall;
Genius gives one apiece to all the rest,
But Shakspeare claims them all!

III.
A Homer, in majestic eloquence,
A Terence, for keen wit and stinging sense,
Brighter than Pindar in his loftiest flight,
Darker than Æschylus for deeds of night,
An Ovid, in the story-pictured page,
A Juvenal, to lash the vicious age,
Graceful as Horace and more skill'd to please,
Tender as pity-stirring Sophocles,
Free as Anacreon, as Martial neat,
Than Virgil's self more delicately sweet,—
O let those ancients bend before Thee now,
And pile their many chaplets on one brow!—

Milton was great, and of divinest song,
Spenser melodious, Chaucer rough and strong,—
The vigorous Dryden, and the classic Gray,
And awful Danté, soaring far away,
Schiller and Göethe, stirring up the strife,
And Molière, dropping laughter into life,
Burns, a full spring of nature, Hood of wit,
And Tennyson, most rare and exquisite,
To each and all belongs the laurell'd crown,
And woe to him who drags their honours down,—
Yet, Shakspeare, thou wert all these lights combined,
O manysided crystal of mankind!

IV.
The jealous Moor, the thoughtful Dane,
The witty rare fat knight,
And grand old Lear half-insane,
And fell Iago's spite,
And Romeo's love, and Tybalt's hate,
And Bolinbroke in regal state,
And he that murdered sleep,—
And ruthless Shylock's bloody bond,
And Prosper with his broken wand
Long buried fathoms deep!
Frank Juliet too,— and that soft pair
Helen and Hermia, lilies fair
As growing on one stem,
Love-crazed Ophelia, drown'd ah! drown'd,
And wanton Cleopatra, crown'd
With Egypt's diadem;
The young Miranda most admired,
Cordelia's filial heart,
Sly Beatrice with wit inspired,
And Ariel's tricksey part,
Fair Rosalind,— sweet banishèd,
And gentle Desdemona — dead!—
Ay these, all these, and crowds beside,
Heroes, jesters, courtiers, clowns,
Girls in grief, or kings in pride,
Threats and crimes, and jokes, and frowns,
Witches, fairies, ghosts, and elves,
All our fancies, all ourselves,—
O! thou hast pictured with thy pen
All phases of all hearts of men,
And in thy various page survives
The Panorama of our lives!

V.
O Paragon unthought before,
O miracle of selftaught lore,
A universe of wit and worth,

The admirable Man of earth,
There is nor thing, nor thought, nor whim,
Untouch'd and unadorn'd by him;
No theme unsung, no truth untold
Of Earth's museum, new or old:
All Nature's hidden things he saw,
Intuitive to every law;
Glancing with supernal scan
At all the knowledge spelt by man;
While, for each rule and craft of Art
He grasp'd it amply, whole and part:
Like travel-wise Ulysses well he knew
Peoples and cities, men and manners too;
With shrewd but ever charitable ken
He read, and wrote out fair, the hearts of men;
Yet, in self-knowledge vers'd, a sage outright,
His giant soul was humble in its might!
O gentle, happy, modest mind,
O genial, cheerful, frank and kind,
Not even could domestic strife
Sour the sweetness of thy life,—
But wheresoe'er thy foot might roam,
Divorced from that Xantipp'd home,
Friends ever found thee,— ay, and foes,
Cordial to these, and kind to those;
Brave, loving, patient, generous, just, and good,—
Beloved by all, our matchless Shakspeare stood!

VI.
Where are thy glorious works unknown?
Who hath not heard thy fame?
On every shore, in every zone,
The World, with glad acclaim,
Yea, from the cottage to the throne,
Hath magnified thy name!
From far Australia to Vancouver's pines,
From the High Alps to Russia's deepest mines,
From China, with her English lesson learnt,
To Chili, wailing for her daughters burnt;
There, everywhere, our Shakspeare breathes and moves
In the sweet ether of all human loves!—
Where rent America now writhes in woe,
Where Nile and Danube, Thames and Ganges flow,
Wherever England sails, and human kind
Anywhere feels in heart, and thinks in mind,
There, everywhere, our Shakspeare's voice is heard,
By him all souls are thrill'd, and cheer'd, and stirr'd;
Each passion flows or ebbs, as Shakspeare speaks,
Hate knits the brow, or terror pales the cheeks,
Love lights the eyes, or pity melts the heart,
And all men bow beneath our Poet's art!

VII.
What monument to rear,
What worthy offering?—
Nought lacks thy glory here
Of all thy sons can bring:
Long since, a twin-sphered brother spake,
How vain it were to raise
To such a Name, for Memory's sake,
Its pyramid of praise:
Our Shakspeare needs no sculptured stones,
No temple for his honoured bones!
But haply in his native street
Beside the rescued home
Hallowed by his infant feet
Whereto all pilgrims roam,
A College well might rear its head,
That Townsman's name to bear,
And brother-actors' sons he bred
To light and learning there!
And, for great London and its throngs,—
To Shakspeare of old right belongs
The Shakspeare Bridge, with Shakspeare scenes
Sculptured upon its pannell'd screens,
Colossus-like the Thames to span,
And telling every passing man
Where a poor player in his youth
Served Heaven and Earth by mimic truth,
And wrapped in Art's and Nature's robe,
Leased,— 'twas his Heritage, — the Globe!—

VIII.
Great Magician for all time,
Denizen of every clime,
Darling poet of mankind,
Master of the human mind,
Nature's very priest and king,—
Take the gifts thy children bring!
Let thy Spirit, hovering o'er
Thine earthly home and haunts of yore,
In its wisdom, wealth, and worth,
Shine upon us from above,
While thy kinsmen here on earth
Thus with pious care and love
Celebrate our Shakspeare's birth.

On The Site of A Mulberry-Tree; Planted By Wm. Shakspeare; Felled By The Rev. F. Gastrell by Dante Gabriel Rossetti

This tree, here fall'n, no common birth or death
Shared with its kind. The world's enfranchised son,
Who found the trees of Life and Knowledge one,
Here set it, frailer than his laurel-wreath.
Shall not the wretch whose hand it fell beneath
Rank also singly—the supreme unhung?
Lo! Sheppard, Turpin, pleading with black tongue
This viler thief's unsuffocated breath!
We'll search thy glossary, Shakspeare! whence almost,
And whence alone, some name shall be reveal'd
For this deaf drudge, to whom no length of ears
Sufficed to catch the music of the spheres;
Whose soul is carrion now,—too mean to yield
Some Starveling's ninth allotment of a ghost.

www.ingramcontent.com/pod-product-compliance
Lightning Source LLC
Chambersburg PA
CBHW071514040426
42444CB00008B/1646